Smart English

A

Workbook and Revision

Units 1-12

REBECCA ROBB BENNE AND ANNA WHITCHER

ROOKEMEAD NGLISH
ANGUAGE EACHING

Smart English A2 Workbook and Revision

Brookemead ELT, London and San Francisco

London, UK

Series editor: Duncan Prowse

Consultant: Mary Tomalin

Designer: Gregor Arthur at Starfish DEPM Ltd

Proofreader: John Bowdler

Audio recordings: John Green at TEFL Audio (producer), Tim Woolf (editor)

Teachers: Thanks to Johanne Skaanes-Allo (Denmark), Viv Blanchard (UK), Emilia Velcheva (Bulgaria), Paul Braddock (Spain), Andrea Krampe (Germany), Neil Kendrick (UK)

San Francisco, USA

Editor and video producer: Anna Whitcher

Illustrators: Carrie English, Aaron Friedland

Video editor: Erin Palmquist

Music: APM Music, Hollywood, California (USA)

Teacher: Thanks to Sophie Abitbol (USA)

Acknowledgements

Cover photo: Anna Whitcher

Unit 1: Carrie English (artwork circus poster; signs); photos: two girls: © Myrleen Pearson / Alamy; sleeping girl: © EPF / Alamy ; twin boys: © Big Cheese Photo LLC / Alamy

Unit 2: Carrie English (artwork places); photos: Rodrigo: Erin Palmquist; Eton: © Peter Titmuss / Alamy; uniform kids: © LondonPhotos - Homer Sykes / Alamy; girl: St. Jude's School, Tanzania

Revision 1-2: photo: two students: Jesper Quistgaard; Carrie English (artwork bulletin board; clocks, places, meals, speeds); Aaron Friedland (artwork subjects)

Unit 3: Carrie English (artwork man; signs; directions; shops); photos: tourist office: © Stuwdamdorp / Alamy; skater: © Daniel Dempster Photography / Alamy; London Eye: © nobleIMAGES / Alamy; Brighton kids; street art: Anna Whitcher

Unit 4: Carrie English (artwork mind map); photos: zip: © ephotocorp / Alamy; Japanese actor: © Jon Arnold Images Ltd / Alamy; fire fighters: San Francisco Fire Department; cross eyes: Erin Palmquist; Lucy: Heydon Prowse

Revision 3-4: photo: Sydney opera house: © David Wall / Alamy; Carrie English (artwork mini maps)

Unit 5: Carrie English (artwork bear, mouths); Aaron Friedland (artwork weather); photos: girl with puppy: © UpperCut Images / Alamy; water boy: © Ian Shaw / Alamy: smiling boy: Erin Palmquist

Unit 6: Carrie English (icons, signs); photos: gadgets: © Bernhard Classen / Alamy; student photos from Paul Braddock's EFL class in Barcelona, Spain; two student photos: Erin Palmquist

Revision 5-6: Carrie English (artwork lady smelling); photo: Winchester Mystery House: © Ambient Images Inc. / Alamy

Unit 7: Carrie English (artwork signs; hand); photos: shopping girls: © David Young-Wolff / Alamy; still from *The world of fashion* video: Heydon Prowse; guitar: © Glowimages RM / Alamy; crossword: www.CrosswordWeaver.com

Unit 8: Carrie English (artwork flags; places to stay; camping gear); photos: boy tourist: © Siegfried Kuttig - RF -2 / Alamy; turtle: © Reinhard Dirscherl / Alamy

Revision 7-8: photos: paradise hotel and four fashion students: Anna Whitcher; girl hiking: © Roger Cracknell 01/classic / Alamy

Unit 9: Carrie English (artwork activity icons; sport icons; skiers); photos: teens talking: © Picture Partners / Alamy; boy dentist: © Dod Miller / Alamy

Unit 10: Carrie English (artwork people cooking; place settings; hamburger boy); photos: student Marie: Anna Whitcher; sitting teen: © OJO Images Ltd / Alamy; still from *A Danish school* video: Jesper Quistgaard

Revision 9-10: photos: student Sam: Heydon Prowse; market: Anna Whitcher; kids in pool: © Christina Kennedy / Alamy; cafeteria food: © Tetra Images / Alamy

Unit 11: Carrie English (artwork art sign); photos: various students: Anna Whitcher; student Shireen: Erin Palmquist; girl studying: © Geomphotography / Alamy; go karts: © Mike Kipling Photography / Alamy

Unit 12: Carrie English (artwork signs; trainers); photos: student Sam: Heydon Prowse; gamer: © Kenny Williamson / Alamy; dolphins: © Charles Stirling (Travel) / Alamy

Revision 11-12: Carrie English (artwork doors, teachers, clocks, DVDs, tests)

Every effort has been made to trace and acknowledge the copyright holders of all the material used in this book. If there any omissions the publishers will be pleased to make the necessary arrangements when the book is reprinted.

Smart English A2

Workbook and Revision (Units 1-12): ISBN **978-1-905248-51-3**

Workbook and Revision CD: ISBN **978-1-905248-52-0**

Also available:

Student's Book (Units 1-12): ISBN 978-1-905248-50-6

Video Pack (Units 1-12) DVD & Worksheets: ISBN 978-1-905248-53-7

Teacher's Guide (Units 1-12)+2 Student Book CDs: ISBN 978-1-905248-59-9

Produced and published by

Brookemead English Language Teaching, London and San Francisco

www.brookemead-elt.co.uk

© Brookemead Associates Ltd, 2012

Contents

Unit Subject	Grammar	Vocabulary / My Words	Communication (A)	Pronunciation (A)	CLIL / Writing	Portfolio writing	Pages
Trinity College, London GESE (Graded Examinations in Spoken English) Grade 3 (Units 1–6), Grade 4 (Units 7–12) Cambridge English KET (Key for Schools) **KET**							
1 Home life	Present simple	Adjectives, daily routines	Getting to know someone, describing daily routines (A)	/s/ /z/ and /ʃ/ (A)	Genetics *About my family*	Email describing home	**4-7**
2 Cool schools	Questions	School, places, subjects, prepositions	Questions to find out personal information (A)	Contractions with question words + *is* (A)	Education *Education in your country*	Information on school website	**8-11**
Revision 1-2							**12-13**
3 Hangouts	Countable and uncountable, *a lot ...*	Hangouts, directions, place prepositions	Talking about your area, asking for and giving directions (A)	/ɒ/ and /əʊ/ (A)	Street art *Describing a picture*	Postcard from a place	**14-17**
4 Not just a job	*can* and *can't*	Jobs, abilities, skills	Talking about skills / ability and inability (A)	Joining sounds (A)	Music industry *Asking about a job*	Asking for information about a summer job	**18-21**
Revision 3-4							**22-23**
5 Scary stories	*was* and *were, and, and then*	Weather, seasons, months, dates, feelings	Talking about weather / a past event (A)	/ɔː/ and /aʊ/ (A)	Moods *Your good and bad moods*	Instant messages about last weekend	**24-27**
6 Tech time	Present continuous	Gadgets, phones, free time	Talking about free time, describing pictures (A)	/tʃ/ and /dʒ/ (A)	Animation *My favourite animation series*	Status on social media page	**28-31**
Revision 5-6							**32-33**
7 Spend or save?	Comparatives and superlatives	Money, clothes, adjectives for clothes	Shopping for clothes, making comparisons (A)	Consonant clusters /st/ and /str/ (A)	Bank accounts *My bank account*	Online adverts to sell old stuff	**34-37**
8 Holidays!	Past simple	Holiday countries, places to stay, travel prepositions	Talking about school holidays / embarrassing holiday moments (A)	/ɪ/ and /iː/ (A)	Ecotourism *A protected area in your country*	Instructions for a hiking trip	**38-41**
Revision 7-8							**42-43**
9 Loves and hates	Like + gerund / infinitive Link word *but*	Hobbies, sports, sports equipment	Talking about favourite sports / likes and dislikes (A)	/ŋ/ (A)	Phobias *Your loves and hates*	Reply to an invitation to a sports event	**44-47**
10 Live to eat?	Adverbs of manner and frequency	Food and drink, adverbs of frequency	Talking about food and drink/ manner and frequency (A)	Intonation of adverbial phrases (A)	Human body *Your health*	Giving food information to a host family	**48-51**
Revision 9-10							**52-53**
11 Learning for life	*going to* future	School and work	Talking about school / future plans (A)	Intonation: tonic stress (A)	Plagiarism *Your tips for writing essays*	Status on social media page	**54-57**
12 Events and experiences	Present perfect with *ever* and *never*	Weekend and seasonal activities	Talking about past events and experiences (A)	Intonation: emphatic stress (A)	Gravity and space *My favourite space story*	Blog comment about summer activities	**58-61**
Revision 11-12							**62-63**
Listening scripts							**64-68**

1 GRAMMAR

The present simple

Use the present simple to talk about routines and habits: *I go to school at 8 o'clock. We have dinner at 6 o'clock.*

Positive			Negative		
I / we / you / they	live	there.	I / we / you / they **don't** (do not)		live there.
he / she / it	live**s**		he / she / it **doesn't** (does not)		
Questions			**Short answers**		
Do I / you / we / they	live	there?	Yes, they **do**. / No, they **don't**.		
Does he / she / it			Yes, she **does**. / No, she **doesn't**.		

A Put in the correct form of the verb.

1 On Sundays we all (get) _____ up late.

2 My dad (make) _____ breakfast.

3 In the afternoon I (hang out) _____ with my friends.

4 My brother (do) _____ his homework.

5 Sometimes my parents (go) _____ shopping.

6 In the evening we (watch) _____ a film or we (play) _____ a game.

SMART TIP

he / she / it + *-s* in positive sentences
I have but *he / she / it has*

B Complete Luiza's sentences. Use negatives.

A Vitaly

1 I live in a city.

2 My family travels a lot.

3 We have a cat.

4 My grandparents live near us.

5 My mum cooks dinner.

6 I like music.

B Luiza

1 *I **don't live** in a city.*

2 My family d _____

3 We _____

4 _____

5 _____

6 _____

C Read the poster. Write the questions and the answers.

CIRCUS SUNRISE

We have clowns, jugglers and lots more!
Performances Wednesdays to Saturdays, 1 pm and 7 pm
Tickets: Adult $28, Child $17

1 what performers / the circus / have?

Q _____

A _____

2 they / perform / at the weekend?

Q _____

A _____

3 what time / the performances / start?

Q _____

A _____

4 how much / a child's ticket / cost?

Q _____

A _____

KET D Circle the best answer for 1–4.

Do you (1) _____ Cirque du Soleil? Every year the circus (2) _____ about 20 different shows. The shows (3) _____ animals, just people. The circus performers (4) _____ from 40 different countries!

1 A knows   B know   C don't know

2 A perform   B doesn't perform   C performs

3 A use   B don't use   C doesn't use

4 A comes   B come   C don't come

2 VOCABULARY

A Write the family members.

Example: Lily is your father's sister. She's your *aunt*.

> half-brother girlfriend ~~aunt~~ grandparents
> boyfriend uncle cousin stepsister

1 Maria is your stepfather's daughter. She's your
_____ .

2 Leon is your aunt's son. He's your _____ .

3 Jerome is your stepmother's and father's son. He's
your _____ .

4 Nadia and Thomas are your mum's mother and
father. They're your _____ .

5 Alma and Huan aren't married. She's his
_____ . He's her _____ .

KET **B** Which notice (A–H) says this (1–5)?

A *Shhh!*
Quiet please!

E Please
keep the
kitchen tidy

B We serve breakfast
7.30 – 9.30
(weekends 10.30)

F The bus goes
at 8.30.
Don't be **late.**

C Please leave
by the same door.

G Children only
with parents

D No school on
Friday 14th

H Fun for
all the family!

1 Please come **early**.   [F]
2 Don't go out a different way.   ☐
3 It isn't boring here.   ☐
4 Don't make this place messy.   ☐
5 Don't be noisy.   ☐

C Look at exercise B again. Underline the pairs of
opposites in the signs and sentences.

Example: 1 early f late

D Match the correct words.

1 have   a music
2 cook   b school
3 listen to   c with friends
4 finish   d dinner
5 get up   e home
6 hang out   f breakfast
7 watch   g early
8 go   h a film

> ### SMART TIP
> Some words often go together with other words.
> They're called collocations.
> Write and learn these words together.

E Complete the time phrases with *in, on* or *at*.

1 Meet me _____ three o'clock.

2 Sorry, I don't have time _____ the weekend.

3 _____ weekdays I go to school.

4 I get up early _____ the morning.

5 Let's watch the film _____ Monday.

6 I go to bed at 10 o'clock _____ the evening.

7 We usually go shopping _____ Saturdays.

8 School finishes at 4 o'clock _____ the afternoon.

MY WORDS FROM UNIT 1

Choose five words you find hard to remember.
Write a sentence for each word or draw a picture.

1 _____
2 _____
3 _____
4 _____
5 _____

Learn them. After Unit 2, check them:
☐ I know these words. ☺
☐ I don't know these words. ☹ (Learn them again!)

3 COMMUNICATION

2 Ⓐ Put the conversation in the correct order (1–6). Then listen and check.

a Yes, he's great. – That's good. ☐

b Do you have brothers and sisters? ☐
  – Yes, two sisters.

c Do you share a room with your sisters? ☐
  – No, I don't. Do you have brothers or sisters?

d I have a sister and a little half-brother. ☐
  – A half-brother?

e How old are they? – Sixteen and eighteen. ☐

f Yes, I live with my mum and my stepfather. ☐
  – Do you like your stepfather?

SMART TIP

Listen to the conversation and then read it out. Practise the questions and answers.

3 Ⓑ 4 ▶ Read the questions and choose the best answer. Then listen to the two conversations and check.

1 What time do you get up?
  A After dinner.
  B Very early.
  C I don't get up.

2 When do you have breakfast?
  A About seven o'clock.
  B I don't know.
  C In the kitchen.

3 What time do you finish school?
  A At three o'clock in the morning.
  B At three o'clock in the afternoon.
  C At three o'clock in the evening.

4 What do you do in the evening?
  A I go to sleep.
  B I get up.
  C I watch TV.

4 PRONUNCIATION

5 Ⓐ Listen to the sounds and words. Say the words.

/s/   /z/   /ʃ/
si**s**ter   brother**s**   **sh**are

6 Ⓑ Listen to the sounds and words in the box. Put them in the correct list.

> Engli**sh**   mu**s**ic   parent**s**   fini**sh**   **s**ixteen
> breakfa**s**t   **sh**ort   hi**s**   cou**s**in
> pronuncia**t**ion   friend**s**   **s**tepfather
> **sh**ower   **s**leep   ea**s**y

/s/

_____

_____

_____

_____

_____

/z/

_____

_____

_____

_____

_____

/ʃ/

_____

_____

_____

_____

_____

6 ⒸListen and check. Then listen again and say the words.

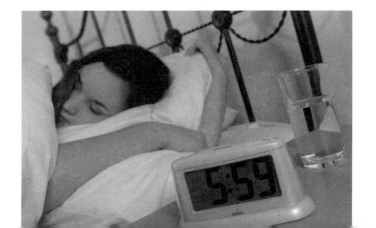

5 CLIL

A Complete the sentences with the correct words.

> DNA   twins   ~~chromosomes~~   personality
> genes   skills   pairs

Human cells have 46 *chromosomes*.

1 There are 23 (1) _____ of chromosomes.

2 The chromosomes contain your (2) _____ .

3 And these contain your (3) _____ .

4 Identical (4) _____ have the same DNA.

5 Your genes decide some of your (5) _____
(what you are like).

6 They also decide some of your (6) _____ .

B Read about Finn's family. Then write four or five sentences about your family. Use phrases from Finn's writing.

> **Me and my family, by Finn**
>
> **I look like** my mum. **We have the same** hair, the same eyes and the same nose. My sister **doesn't look like anybody in our family**. But my brother **looks like** my dad. **They're** tall and have the same ears!

Me and my family, by _____

_____

_____

_____

_____

_____

6 PORTFOLIO WRITING

A Read Amelie's email. True (T) or false (F)?

Amelie ...
1 lives with her parents. ☐
2 has a big sister. ☐
3 lives in a house. ☐
4 gets up before 7. ☐
5 goes to bed very late. ☐

Quick links		Search mail	

Dear Julia

I live with my mum, brother and sister in Paris. I'm 14. My little brother is 10 and my sister is 15. We have an apartment with four rooms. It has a small balcony. I share a bedroom with my sister.

We get up at 7.15 on weekdays and school starts at 8.30. I go to bed about 10 o'clock.

Write soon!

Amelie

SMART TIP

When you write an email, start and finish like Amelie.
You can also use *Hi* to start and *Bye* to finish.

B What words does Amelie use to:

1 start the email?

_____

2 finish the email?

_____

C You are Julia. Write an email to Amelie
KET (40–60 words). Tell her:

– about your family
– about your home
– about your day

SMART TIP

Always read your writing and check it.

1 GRAMMAR: Questions

In questions, we change the order of the person (*he*) and the verb (*is*).
In present simple questions, we use *do/does* + person. We use *do/does* in short answers too.

Positive	Question	Short answers
be He **is** fourteen.	**Is** he fourteen?	Yes, he is. / No, he isn't.
Present simple I / You / We / They **like** school. He / She / It **likes** school.	**Do** you **like** school? **Does** she **like** school?	Yes, I do. / No, I don't. Yes, she does. / No, she doesn't.

We put question words at the beginning of a question.

time	***When / What time*** *do you start school?*	a reason	***Why*** *do you like history?*
a place	***Where*** *do you live?*	a number	***How many*** *students are at your school?*
a person	***Who*** *is your teacher?*	in what way	***How*** *do you go to school?*
a thing	***What*** *do you do after school?*		

A Read the conversation with Rodrigo. Write questions for him.

1 Where _____?
   I go to Burlingame High School in California.

2 Are _____?
   Yes, there are a lot – over 1,400 students.

3 Is _____?
   Yes, it is, it's a very good school.

4 Does _____?
   Yes, it does, it has a big swimming pool.

5 What _____?
   After classes? I usually do sport.

SMART TIP

In questions the main verb always has the same form.
*Do you **like**? Does he **like**? (X Does he ~~likes~~?)*

B Choose the best word for each question.

1 _____ is your school?
   a When   b Where   c Why

2 _____ do you go to school?
   a Who   b What   c How

3 _____ students are there in your class?
   a How   b How many   c Where

4 _____ do you sit with in class?
   a What   b Who   c When

5 _____ do / don't you like your school?
   a Why   b What   c How many

C Complete the email. Write one word for each space.

Quick links		Search mail	

Hi, Carlos

Tell me more about your school! Is (1) _____ a big school? How (2) _____ students are there? What class (3) _____ you in? (4) _____ is your favourite subject? (5) _____ you like history? I don't like history!

What about sport? (6) _____ the school have a football team?

Jake

2 VOCABULARY

A Read and (circle) the correct answers.

Eton College is a very (1) *old / new* school – it's from 1440. There are about 1,300 students, so it's quite (2) *big / small*. The school isn't open to everybody – it's a (3) *public / private* school and it's only for boys. The school is very expensive and most boys come from (4) *rich / poor* families. Students wear (5) *normal clothes / a uniform*: everybody wears traditional black clothes.

B Write the correct school places.

classroom	cinema	tennis court	gym
cafeteria	~~library~~	football pitch	main hall

1 *library*　2 _____　3 _____　4 _____

5 _____　6 _____　7 _____　8 _____

SMART TIP

Draw small pictures with words and learn them together.

C Write the school subjects for the definitions.

Example: You learn about places.　　*geography*

1 You learn about animals and people. b_____

2 You move about and play games.　　s_____

3 You learn about important events.　h_____

4 You draw and paint pictures.　　　a_____

5 You learn about things like light and sound.　　　　　　　　　p_____

6 You learn to use numbers.　　　　m_____

D Put in the correct prepositions.

by (x2)	for (x2)	from	in (x2)
of (x2)	to (x2)	with	

1 The name _____ our school is Hallcross High School.

2 Our school is _____ students _____ 11 _____ 16.

3 Most students go _____ school _____ bus.

4 There are thirty students _____ each class.

5 We call our teachers _____ their last names.

6 We usually work _____ small groups _____ five students.

7 We work _____ computers and books.

8 We don't pay _____ books and other school things.

SMART TIP

Learn prepositions with other words and phrases.

E Match the words to make collocations.

1 have	a kayaking
2 wear	b Spanish
3 go	c clothes
4 take	d people
5 make	e classes
6 play	f photos
7 speak	g cards
8 meet	h films

MY WORDS FROM UNIT 2

1 _____

2 _____

3 _____

4 _____

5 _____

After Unit 3:

☐ I know these words. ☺

☐ I don't know these words. ☹ (Learn them again!)

3 COMMUNICATION

7 ▶ A Complete the conversation. Write the correct letters (A–G) for 1–5. There are two extra sentences. Then listen and check.

Girl I see you're at Churchill School.
Boy (1) *E*
Girl Your uniform! Do you like it there?
Boy (2) _____
Girl I go to Westpark High.
Boy (3) _____
Girl Yeah, that's right. I like it there.
Boy (4) _____
Girl Yes, the classrooms and everything are all new.
Boy (5) _____
Girl Yes, they're OK.

A No. I'm not.
B It looks nice, very modern.
C Are the teachers nice?
D Are there a lot of students?
E ~~How do you know that?~~
F Well, not the uniform! But yes, it's OK.
G Right, is that the new school near the park?

8 ▶ B Cross out the answer that is NOT correct.
9 ▶ Then listen to the two conversations and check.

1 Where are you from?
   From Italy. / It's a town. / I'm English.
2 Where do you live?
   In the library. / About two kilometres from here.
   / Near the school.
3 How do you go to school?
   I walk. / By bus. / At 8 o'clock.
4 Do you like school?
   No, I don't. / We go kayaking. / It's OK.
5 What's your favourite subject?
   IT / breakfast / geography

4 PRONUNCIATION

10 ▶ A In English we often put question words and *is* together when we speak. Listen to the questions. Repeat them.

1 **What is** your name?
   What's your name?
2 **Where is** your school?
   Where's your school?
3 **Who is** your favourite teacher?
   Who's your favourite teacher?
4 **When is** the English lesson?
   When's the English lesson?

10 ▶ B Listen again to the questions in A.
In *is* the sound is /z/.

In *What's / Where's / Who's / When's* the sound changes from /z/ to /s/ in one word. Which word? Listen again and (circle) it.

11 ▶ C Put the correct words in the speech bubbles. Then listen and check.

1 _____ best friend?

2 _____ your birthday?

3 _____ your house?

4 _____ your phone number?

11 ▶ D Listen again to the questions in C and repeat.

SMART TIP

Try and use words like *What's / Where's / Why's* in speaking (but not in writing).

5 CLIL

A Read the text. Then write the words for the meanings below.

Help us – become a sponsor!

Our education is free for students – but we need sponsors. Education is very important here in Tanzania. Some families live on only $2 a day. If students finish primary and secondary education, they can help their family. The language of university courses is English and not Kiswahili, the Tanzanian language. So at our school, classes and exams are in English.

1 he or she pays for somebody's education

   _____

2 you don't pay

   _____

3 education for young students

   _____

4 education for older students

   _____

5 where you study when you finish school

   _____

6 an important test

   _____

B Write about education in your country. Use the questions to help you.

   – Is education important or not so important?
   – Is primary education free?
   – Is secondary education free?
   – What language do you speak in your school classes?
   – Do you think students get a good education?

   Education is _____

   _____

   _____

   _____

   _____

6 PORTFOLIO WRITING

A Read the information for new students on a school website. Complete the notes.

Welcome to our school!
• Redwood School is a small school. There are about 350 students.
• There are two classes in each year. There are about 30 students in each class.
• All students wear a uniform. Our school uniform is grey and white.
• School starts at 8.45 and finishes at 3.05. Lunch is from 12.00 to 1.00 in the cafeteria.
• The school office is near the main door. It's open from 8.00 to 4.00.
• Our headteacher is Mrs Wilson. Her office is near the library.
See you at Redwood!

Students in school: _____

Students in class: _____

Uniform colours: _____

School hours: _____

Lunch times: _____

Office times: _____

Headteacher's name: _____

B Find the phrases with these meanings.

1 We are happy to tell you about our school.

   _____

2 We would like to see you at our school.

   _____

KET C Write some information for new students about your school (80–100 words). Use the information and phrases in A to help you. Say:

   – how big the school and classes are
   – what school uniform or clothes students wear
   – when school starts and finishes and what time lunch is
   – where the school office and the headteacher's office are

1 GRAMMAR

A Complete the text with the correct form of the verb.

At Henriette Hørlücks School, school (1 *start*) _____ at 8.15. But students (2 *not begin*) _____ classes at 8.15. They (3 *go*) _____ to a meeting of all the students first. They (4 *sing*) _____ and the headteacher usually (5 *play*) _____ some music too. This (6 *not take*) _____ very long – about 15 minutes. Students (7 *have*) _____ classes and then they (8 *eat*) _____ lunch at 11 o'clock. Students (9 *not have*) _____ many classes in the afternoon. For most students, school (10 *finish*) _____ at 14.05.

B Put the words in the questions in the right order. Write short answers.

1 have / do / brothers and sisters / you? (✗)
_____

2 work / your parents / do? (✓)
_____

3 your flat / does / a balcony / have? (✓)
_____

4 you / live / does / near / your friend Anna? (✗)
_____

5 you / do / people in your family / look like? (✗)
_____

C Write the questions with the correct question words from the box. Write your answers.

| What   How many   What time   When |
| How   Why |

1 you / get up? _____
_____

2 you / go to school? _____

3 classes / you / have / in one day?_____

4 classes / you / like? _____

5 you / like / them? _____
_____

6 do / you / have / these classes? _____
_____

2 VOCABULARY

A In the word search (→ ↓ ↘ ↗), find five words each for:

family   adjectives (describing words)

places in a school   school subjects

S	L	F	N	E	W	L	I	B	R	A	R	Y
D	T	B	F	C	H	E	M	I	S	T	R	Y
M	G	E	J	H	T	Y	D	R	R	A	R	T
W	R	B	P	K	I	R	J	E	M	S	Z	P
C	A	M	Q	F	A	S	T	Z	C	M	W	L
A	N	F	W	H	A	H	T	I	N	A	M	A
F	D	C	K	H	G	T	S	O	N	L	A	Y
E	M	N	I	U	B	Y	H	I	R	L	T	G
T	O	R	A	N	H	O	S	E	K	Y	H	R
E	T	D	I	P	E	U	R	M	R	R	S	O
R	H	N	L	C	O	M	Y	I	N	Y	N	U
I	E	T	T	C	H	G	A	F	N	K	N	N
A	R	D	P	A	R	E	N	T	S	G	Y	D

B Make two collocations for each verb (a–e). Complete the sentences (1–5) with one collocation.

| home   in the playground   work   early |
| classes   to bed   school   with friends |
| breakfast   late |

a have _____ / _____

b get up _____ / _____

c hang out _____ / _____

d go _____ / _____

e finish _____ / _____

1 We always _____ at 7 am in the kitchen.

2 At the weekend I _____ about 11 am.

3 At school the small kids _____.

4 I _____ at 10 pm.

5 My parents _____ about 5 pm.

C Complete the notes with the correct prepositions.

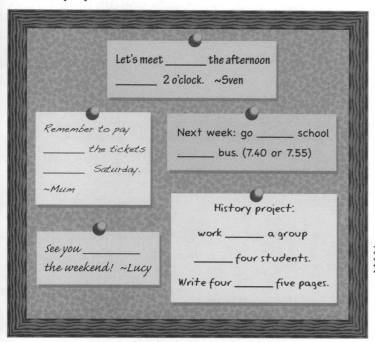

Let's meet _____ the afternoon _____ 2 o'clock. ~Sven

Remember to pay _____ the tickets _____ Saturday. ~Mum

Next week: go _____ school _____ bus. (7.40 or 7.55)

History project: work _____ a group _____ four students. Write four _____ five pages.

See you _____ the weekend! ~Lucy

3 LISTENING KET

13 Listen to five short conversations. There is one question for each conversation.
For questions 1-5, tick (✓) under the right answer.

1 What time does school start?

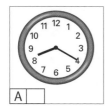 A
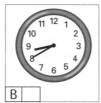 B
 C

2 Where does the boy live?

 A
 B
 C

3 When does the girl NOT eat a lot?

 A
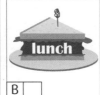 B
 C

4 How far is the girl's new flat?

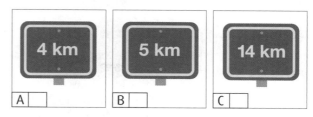

A | B | C

4 km | 5 km | 14 km

5 What's the boy's favourite subject?

 A
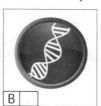 B
 C

$2x^3 = y$

4 READING KET

Read the text about a circus school. Are sentences 1–6 right (A) or wrong (B)?
If the text doesn't say this information, write doesn't say (C).

GO TO CIRCUS SCHOOL!

Do you sometimes think 'I'd like to be in a circus'? Well, it's easy – just find a circus school! There are 680 circus schools in 52 different countries – that's a lot!

Circus Space is one of these schools. It's a circus school in London for young people and adults. At *Circus Space*, young people from 11-21 years learn to be circus performers. They do classes for two hours a week on Sundays at the *Circus Space* school. *Circus Space* has a big building in north London with two large training halls and a library. Students do lots of different circus activities: for example, they learn to be jugglers and trapeze artists. Students perform in real circus shows too. For students over eighteen, *Circus Space* also has university circus courses.

1 There aren't many circus schools.
   A Right   B Wrong   C Doesn't say
2 Circus Space is a school in the UK.
   A Right   B Wrong   C Doesn't say
3 It's expensive to do classes at Circus Space.
   A Right   B Wrong   C Doesn't say
4 Classes at Circus Space are at the weekend.
   A Right   B Wrong   C Doesn't say
5 Circus Space's building is very modern.
   A Right   B Wrong   C Doesn't say
6 Students only learn to be jugglers.
   A Right   B Wrong   C Doesn't say

1 GRAMMAR

Countable and uncountable

We use *a / an* and plural *-s* with **countable** words. Examples:
place, city, park, street, tree, building, shop, road, bank, organisation, area, problem

We DON'T use *a / an* and plural *–s* with **uncountable** words. Examples:
traffic, money, water, information, violence, litter, crime, graffiti, food, help, homework, education

countable	uncountable
place – a place, some places area – an area, some areas	traffic – some traffic, a traffic, some traffics money – some money, a money, some monies

A lot (++), much (++), many (++), some (+), any (0)

- We use **a lot (of)** with countable and uncountable words.
  There is a lot of traffic in our city: a lot of cars and buses.

- We use ***many*** with countable words and ***much*** with uncountable words.
  We usually use these in questions and negative sentences.
  How much traffic is there? Well, there aren't many cars, but there are a lot of buses.

- We use ***some*** and ***any*** with countable and uncountable words.
  We usually use **some** in positive sentences, and **any** in questions and negative sentences.
  Let's buy some bottles of water. – Oh, sorry, I don't have any money. Do you have any money?

- But we use *some* in questions when we want to offer something.
  Would you like some water?

A **Complete the dialogues with *a / an* or *some*.**

1 We need _____ information about the area.
   – I think there's _____ information office here.

2 Let's ask that woman for _____ help.
   – OK. Then let's buy _____ map.

3 I need _____ money.
   – There's _____ bank
   over there.

4 Let's buy _____ food
   in the supermarket.
   – OK, there's _____
   park. We can eat there.

Tourist
Information

B **Your parents want to buy an apartment. Complete what the man says about the area. Use *a lot of, much, many*. (Sometimes two answers are correct.)**

1 How _____ shops are there?
   Oh, there are _____ shops.

2 Yes, there are _____ trees.

3 No, there isn't _____ litter.

4 Yes, there are _____ things for teenagers.

5 Yes, there are _____ restaurants.

6 No, there isn't _____ graffiti.

C **You and your parents look at the apartment in exercise B. Choose the correct word.**

1 There aren't *some / any* shops.

2 There aren't *some / any* trees.

3 There is *some / any* litter.

4 Are there *some / any* things for teenagers?

5 There aren't *some / any* restaurants.

6 There is *some / any* graffiti.

SMART TIP

Some words (like *information*) are **U**ncountable in English but **C**ountable in other languages.
Look in a dictionary for **U** or **C** next to the word.

2 VOCABULARY

A Answer the questions with the correct word from the box.

café   beach   skate park
library   park   online
shopping centre
my friend's house
swimming pool

1   Which word isn't a real place? _____

2   Where can you buy clothes? _____

3   Which two places can you go in the water?
_____ and _____

4   Where can you hang out together, watch TV and lots of other things? _____

5   Where can you do the sport in the picture?
_____

6   Where can you sit and have a drink? _____

7   Where is there grass and trees? _____

8   Where are there a lot of books? _____

KET **B** Match the signs (1–6) to six of the places. There are two extra.

1
Please
do not touch
the pictures.

4
Fast trains.
Please stand back.

2
Next performance
Tuesday 7th, 20.00
Ticket office
open daily 15–20.00

5
Please wait
here for a table.

3
Visitors: stop!
Wash your hands
with soap and water.

6
Please use
the machines outside
for amounts under £200.

A bank   B hospital   C theatre
D police station E museum   F hotel
G train station   H restaurant

C Complete the directions. Use the pictures and the words in the box.

straight on   across   past   up
along   down   right   left

1
Turn _____ and go _____ the hill.

2
Go _____ the street and turn _____

3
Go _____ and go _____ the hill.

4
Go _____ the street and go _____ the bank.

D Look at the picture. (Circle) the correct prepositions.

1   There's a clothes shop *in front of / between* a music shop and a book shop.
2   *Opposite / Next to* the book shop is a fruit shop.
3   There's some litter in *front of / behind* the shops.
4   There are some trees *behind / next to* the shops.
5   There is some grass *between / opposite* the shops.

MY WORDS FROM UNIT 3

1   _____
2   _____
3   _____
4   _____
5   _____

After Unit 4:
☐ I know these words. ☺
☐ I don't know these words. ☹ (Learn them again!)

3 COMMUNICATION

12 ▶ A Willow is talking about hangouts. What does she say next? Choose A, B or C. Then listen and check.

1 I often hang out at the shopping mall.
  A I don't like it there.
  B There are a lot of things to do.
  C It's really boring.

2 I usually hang out with school friends.
  A I'm happy on my own.
  B My parents come with me.
  C But sometimes I hang out with my sister.

3 I sometimes go to the cinema.
  A But I never watch films.
  B The tickets are too expensive.
  C But only when there is a good film.

4 I often hang out with my friends online.
  A We chat on Facebook.
  B We do our homework.
  C I meet my boyfriend.

13 ▶ B
14 ▶ Read sentences (a–f). They are lines from two conversations. Write each conversation in the correct order. Then listen and check.

a Where's Queen Street?
b Go straight on and turn right at the cinema. The bank is on the left.
c How do I get to King's Road?
d Go past the library and turn left. The police station is on the right.
e It's in Queen Street.
f Yes, there's one in King's Road.

Conversation 1

A Excuse me, how do I get to the police station?
B 1 _____
A 2 _____
B 3 _____
A Thank you.

Conversation 2

A Excuse me, is there a bank near here?
B 4 _____
A 5 _____
B 6 _____
A Thank you.

4 PRONUNCIATION

15 ▶ A Listen to the sounds and words. Say the words.

/ɒ/ and /əʊ/

problem   go
boxing   show

SMART TIP

Learn the symbols with the sounds.
Then you can check the pronunciation of new words in your dictionary.

16 ▶ B Listen to the sounds and words in the box. Put them in the correct list.

online hospital clothes across hotel
problem postcard home know opposite
role office photo offer kilometre over

/ɒ/   /əʊ/

_____   _____
_____   _____
_____   _____
_____   _____
_____   _____
_____   _____
_____   _____
_____   _____

16 ▶ C Listen and check. Then listen again and say the words.

5 CLIL

KET A Read and choose the best word for each space.

> Street art is often against the (1) _____ but there are special street art projects. Vanessa Solari Espinoza is an (2) _____ and teacher in California, USA. Vanessa teaches students to create their own (3) _____. They learn different kinds of street art: graffiti (4) _____ (the artist's name), (5) _____ pictures, stencils and (6) _____ art. Through art students learn to (7) _____ how they feel.

1	A wall	B	law	C	building
2	A artist	B	organisation	C	area
3	A problems	B	violence	C	style
4	A words	B	tags	C	people
5	A spray-paint	B	water	C	litter
6	A face	B	traffic	C	sticker
7	A think	B	communicate	C	hang out

B Write about the picture.

What is there in the picture?
There are ... / There is ... / I see ...
buildings / a face with ...

Why do you like it or not like it?
I like it / don't like it because ...
... it's funny / interesting / a good piece of art.

Do you like street art?
I like / don't like street art because ...

_____
_____
_____
_____
_____
_____

6 PORTFOLIO WRITING

A Read Sam's postcard. Choose the correct words.

1 Sam is on *a family visit / a school trip*.
2 He *likes / doesn't like* London.
3 He thinks the buildings, parks and shops are *OK / really good*.
4 The restaurants have *English / lots of different* food.
5 Sam is *happy / bored* in London.

Hi Ellen

I'm in London with my class. It's a great city! There are a lot of beautiful buildings and big parks. The shops are fantastic too. And there are wonderful restaurants and cafés with food from all over the world. I love it here – there are a lot of different people and things to do.

Love Sam

B Which four words in the postcard mean *very good* or *very nice*? Write them here.

_____   _____

_____   _____

C Think of an interesting place. Write a postcard to
KET an English friend (40–60 words). Tell your friend:

– where you are
– what there is there and what the place is like
– why you like the place

1 GRAMMAR

Can and can't

We use **can** + verb to talk about ability (skills we have).
I can work in a team.
We use **can't** (can not) + verb to talk about inability (skills we don't have).
I can't drive a car.

We use **can / can't** to talk about permission – things it is OK or not OK to do.
We can drink water in class.
We can't eat in class.

Positive	Negative	Question	Short answers
I **can** drive.	I **can't** drive.	**Can** you drive?	Yes, I can. / No, I can't.

A Look at Jin's answers to a magazine questionnaire. Write about her. Use *can* and *can't*.

How active are you? Can you ...	
1 swim?	✓
2 scuba dive?	✗
3 dance?	✓
4 play football?	✗
5 ride a horse?	✗
6 do martial arts?	✓

1 Jin can _____

2 She _____

3 _____

4 _____

5 _____

6 _____

SMART TIP

In questions with *can*, we don't use *do*.

B Now write your answers to the questionnaire.

1 _____

2 _____

3 _____

4 _____

5 _____

6 _____

C Complete Alex Rider's spy tips with *can* or *can't*.

1 Put hairs in the zip of a bag. So you _____ see when somebody opens it.

2 Use a skateboard. You _____ move really fast on this.

3 Put your jacket over an angry dog's head, so the dog _____ see.

4 Use a different name so people _____ find you.

5 You _____ use your clothes to make a fire.

6 Use bright lights in people's eyes, so they _____ see you at night.

D Complete the classroom dialogues between student (S) and teacher (T). Write the questions. Then complete the answers with *can / can't*.

1 **S** _____ to the toilet?　　　　(I / go)

　T Yes, you _____ . But be quick!

2 **T** _____ the exercise?　　(you / finish)

　S We _____ do it. It's too hard.

3 **S** _____ dictionaries?　　　(we / use)

　T Sorry, no, you _____ use them in tests.

4 **T** _____ the text please?　　(you / read)

　S I _____ find my book.

5 **S** _____ to that again?　　(we / listen)

　T Yes, we _____ . Just a moment.

2 VOCABULARY

A Write the correct jobs for the definitions.

1 I work in a hospital but I'm not a doctor:

    n _____

2 I work in a restaurant: w _____ / w _____

3 I work in a shop: s _____

4 I have a farm: f _____

5 I work in a theatre: a _____

6 I work with machines: e _____

7 I work at a police station: p _____

8 I visit different places: e _____

B Choose the best word to complete the sentences.

confident	friendly	clever
brave	creative	calm

1 Artists are _____

2 University teachers are _____

3 A good shop assistant is _____

4 Explorers and police officers are _____

5 Actors and pop stars are _____

6 Good nurses and doctors are _____

C Look at the words in the box. Write them next to the correct verbs in the mind map.

a horse	Japanese	mountains	a plane
French	a quad bike	German	
a car	martial arts	a mountain bike	

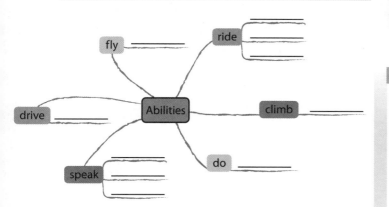

SMART TIP

Draw a mind map to learn words.

D Read about Camp Blaze. Choose the best word
KET for each space.

Example: (0)   A work   B job   C training

The girls at Camp Blaze are in (0) _____. They want
to be (1) _____. The girls learn to
(2) _____ fires. They also learn about accidents,
medical (3) _____ and fire (4) _____. They
work together in a (5) _____. They can carry heavy
(6) _____ and stay (7) _____ in dangerous
situations. These girls can (8) _____ your life!

1	A	actors	B	fire fighters	C doctors
2	A	start	B	finish	C put out
3	A	camps	B	emergencies	C mountains
4	A	safety	B	government	C danger
5	A	room	B	factory	C team
6	A	furniture	B	equipment	C horses
7	A	tired	B	calm	C dead
8	A	give	B	find	C save

MY WORDS FROM UNIT 4

1 _____

2 _____

3 _____

4 _____

5 _____

After Unit 5:

☐ I know these words. ☺

☐ I don't know these words. ☹ (Learn them again!)

3 COMMUNICATION

17 Ⓐ **Put the conversations in the correct order.**
18 **Write 1, 2, 3, 4 in the boxes.**
19 **Then listen and check.**

1 a What sort of work does she do? ☐
   b What does your mum do? ☐
   c Tests and things like that. ☐
   d She works at a hospital. ☐

2 a No, he has an office in town. ☐
   b Cool. Does he work at home? ☐
   c He's a writer. He writes for a magazine. ☐
   d What does your dad do? ☐

3 a No, he doesn't. ☐
   b He'd like to be an engineer. ☐
   c Does your brother have a job? ☐
   d What does he want to do? ☐

20 Ⓑ **Match the questions and answers.**
Then listen and check.

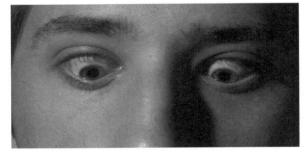

1 Can you cross your eyes? – Yes, I can.
   A It's dangerous.   B It's funny.
   C It's friendly.

2 Can you stand on your head? – Yes, I can.
   A But not for long.   B For two months.
   C It's for my sister.

3 Can you sing? – No, I can't.
   A I'm a pop star.   B I sound horrible.
   C I follow instructions.

4 Can you do martial arts? – No I can't.
   A My eyes are blue.   B I'm tall.
   C I'm not good at sport.

5 Can you tell jokes? – Yes, I can.
   A I'm a spy.
   B Do you know the one about the farmer?
   C I don't like them.

6 Can you eat five pizzas? – No, I can't.
   A And I don't want to do this.
   B I love pizza.   C I want to work with animals.

4 PRONUNCIATION

21 Ⓐ **Listen to the sentences. Listen to how the sounds join together. Then listen again and repeat.**

She's‿a writer.
He's‿an‿explorer.

22 Ⓑ **Listen and join the sounds together. Then listen again and repeat.**

1 He's a police officer.
2 She's an engineer.
3 He's a farmer.
4 She's a doctor.
5 He's a teacher.
6 She's a cleaner.
7 He's a driver.
8 She's an actor.

23 Ⓒ **Now listen to these sentences and repeat.**

1 She works‿at‿a hospital.
2 He works‿in‿an‿office.

24 Ⓓ **Listen and join the sounds together. Then listen again and repeat.**

1 She works in a theatre.
2 I work in a factory.
3 They work at a police station.
4 He works at a school.
5 They work in a restaurant.
6 We work on a farm.

5 CLIL

A Write the words for the definitions.

1 You get these on the internet – sometimes for free.
d_____

2 These are the words of a song.
l_____

3 You can buy music in shops on these.
c_____ d_____ (CD)

4 This is when you make a CD/DVD in a studio.
r_____

5 The tickets for these events are often expensive.
c_____

B Complete the interview with the correct jobs.

roadie	sound engineer	manager
producer	tour manager	A&R

Interviewer How do bands and singers get into the music industry?

Lucy Well, that's my job. I'm an (1) _____. I look for new artists on the internet or at clubs and festivals.

Interviewer What other jobs are there?

Lucy The artist usually has a (2)_____. He or she organises the artist's career.

Interviewer But there's also a (3) _____?

Lucy Yes, they organise live concerts in different places. Lots of different people work for them. A (4) _____, for example, gets all the equipment in order.

Interviewer And there are jobs in the studio too?

Lucy Yes, the (5) _____ helps the artist with the recording. And the (6) _____ does the sound.

6 PORTFOLIO WRITING

A Read about the job and Matthew's email. Complete the sentences.

1 Matthew is interested in _____

2 He wants more _____

3 He asks about the days and the _____

> **Lemontree Restaurant**
> We need a waiter / waitress for summer weekends. Start next month.
> Please contact Diane Williams diane@lemontree.com

> Dear Ms Williams
>
> I am very interested in the job as a waiter in your restaurant. Can you please give me some more information? Is it for Saturday and Sunday every week? What are the work hours each day?
>
> I look forward to hearing from you.
>
> Yours sincerely
>
> Matthew Jennings

SMART TIP

For a woman, use *Ms* and her family name. For a man, use *Mr*.

B Match the phrases with their use.

1 *Dear ...*   a to ask for a reply
2 *Can you please give me*   b to finish the email
3 *I look forward to hearing from you*   c to start the email
4 *Yours sincerely*   d to ask for information

C Now read about this job. Write an email for
KET more information (40–60 words).

> **THE PET CENTRE**
> We need a shop assistant for the summer.
> 20 hours a week.
> Please contact Rashid Abdur thepetcentre@mail.com

Ask:
– what animals they have in the shop
– what days the job is
– when the job starts

1 GRAMMAR

A Complete the information about Sydney, Australia. Choose the correct word.

Sydney is on the Tasman Sea, (1) *a / some* part of the Pacific Ocean. There are (2) *a lot of / any* beaches in and near Sydney. There are also (3) *any / some* mountains (The Blue Mountains) to the west of the city. Visitors can eat (4) *a / some* really good food in Sydney's cafés and restaurants. It's (5) *a / some* safe city and there isn't (6) *a / any* real crime. Most tourists don't have (7) *any / some* problems but you can find (8) *an / some* information on the internet about how to stay safe.

B Complete these questions with *much* or *many*. Then match them to the correct answers (a–f).

Sydney Opera House and Sydney Harbour Bridge

1 How _____ square kilometres (km²) is Sydney? ☐
2 How _____ people live there? ☐
3 How _____ sun does Sydney get? ☐
4 How _____ water is in the Pacific Ocean? ☐
5 How _____ rooms does the Sydney Opera house have? ☐
6 How _____ time does it take to walk over Sydney Harbour Bridge? ☐

   a 4 million
   b half an hour
   c about 7 hours a day
   d 4,000
   e 1,000
   f 46% of the world's water

C Complete the dialogue with *can* or *can't*.

Mum It's a nice day again. We (1) _____ go to the beach.

Tim We (2) _____ go to the beach again! That's boring!

Mum Well, (3) _____ you look in the guide book?

Tim OK ... Hey, (4) _____ we walk over the Harbour Bridge?

Mum I (5) _____ walk much today. I'm too tired.

Dad I know, we (6) _____ go to the Art Museum.

Tim No, we (7) _____.

Mum Why not?

Tim You (8) _____ visit the museum on Mondays. It's closed.

2 VOCABULARY

A Who is the person? Write the job (a). Where is the person? Write the place (b).

1 'You are so beautiful ... I love you so much.'
   a ac_____ b th_____

2 'Where does it hurt?'
   a d_____ b h_____

3 'So, you want to report some graffiti on your building?'
   a p_____ o_____ b p_____ s_____

4 'Here you are, two pizzas.'
   a w_____ b r_____

5 'What's the problem with this machine?'
   a e_____ b f_____

6 'Two DVDs? That's £18, please.'
   a s_____ a_____ b s_____ ce_____

B Circle the odd word out.

Example: plane, bike, ⬭mountain, car

1 exciting, fun, boring, cool
2 French, America, German, Japanese
3 strict, dangerous, hard, quiet
4 speak, drive, ride, fly
5 brave, calm, scared, confident

C **Complete the directions with the correct words.**

| straight on | past | between | along | next to |
| left | behind | opposite | right | in front of |

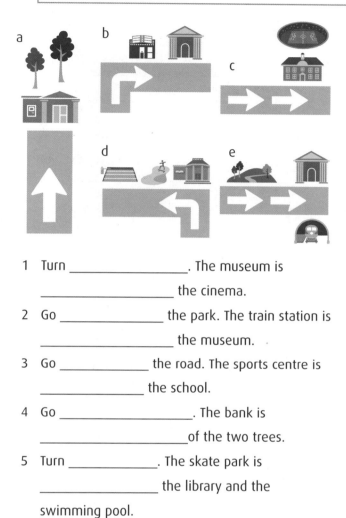

1 Turn _____. The museum is
_____ the cinema.

2 Go _____ the park. The train station is
_____ the museum.

3 Go _____ the road. The sports centre is
_____ the school.

4 Go _____. The bank is
_____ of the two trees.

5 Turn _____. The skate park is
_____ the library and the
swimming pool.

26 ▶ **Listen to Lucy talking about her family's jobs. What job does each person do?**

For questions 1–5, write the name of a job (A–H) next to each person. There are three extra jobs.

People

1 Mum ☐
2 Dad ☐
3 Ben ☐
4 Gina ☐
5 Alice ☐

Jobs

A cleaner
B shop assistant
C driver
D doctor
E police officer
F engineer
G nurse
H fire fighter

---

4 READING **KET**

Read the email and the website information about the job. Complete the job form for Lucas.

noahw@post.com

To: lucask@bwt.com

Hi Lucas

There's a job for a dog walker at Plus Pet Services. It's a great job for you because you love dogs. I know you play football on Saturdays. But there was something after school one day. (There's also a job in the shop but you can't do that because you're only 15.) Look at their website.

Noah

Plus Pet Services

Shop assistant

Do you like animals? Are you 16 or over? We need a shop assistant for Saturday mornings in our shop in High Street in Norton (8am–1pm).

Dog walkers

Do you like dogs? Are you 15 or over? We need dog walkers for Thursdays and Saturdays, morning (10 am) and afternoon (4 pm).

Job application form

Name:	Lucas King
Email address:	
Age:	
Job:	
Day / time you can work:	
Why you would like this job:	

1 GRAMMAR

The past simple of *be*: *was* and *were*

We use *was* and *were* to talk about states in the past.
*It **was** cold yesterday.*
*We **weren't** at school last week.*

PAST   NOW

Last week   Yesterday   Today

Positive		Negative	
I / he / she /it **was** we / you / they **were**	at home.	I / he / she /it **wasn't** (was not) we / you / they **weren't** (were not)	at home.
Questions		**Short answers**	
Was I / he / she / it **Were** you / we / they	at home?	Yes, I was. / No, I wasn't. Yes, they were. / No they weren't.	

We can use these time phrases with *was / were:*
yesterday   last (week / month / year)   in 2010   in the (twentieth / twenty-first) century

and / and then
We use **and** to link two ideas or events.
It was dark and I was alone at home.
We use **and then** to show two events happen one after another.
There was a big storm and then there weren't any lights.

Ⓐ Complete the story with *was* and *were*.

One day a visitor (1) _____ in a bedroom in the Queen's
House at the Tower. Suddenly, there (2) _____ strong
hands on the vistor's neck ... but she (3) _____ alone
in the room. People say the hands (4) _____ those
of Arbella Stuart's ghost. Arbella Stuart (5) _____
a cousin of King James I. From 1610 to 1615, she
(6) _____ a prisoner in this room.

**Ⓑ Write another story about the Tower. Use the
words below and *was / wasn't, were / weren't*.**

1 (In 1241, / there / a bear / at the Tower)

_____

2 (Many years later, / there / a big white bear / at
the Tower)

_____

3 (But it / not a real / bear – it / a ghost)

_____

4 (The guards / very scared)

_____

5 (But after that, / there / not / any more stories
about the bear)

_____

**Ⓒ Complete the conversation. Write the questions
and complete the short answers.**

A (1 where / be / you)

_____ yesterday?

B I was at my grandparents' house.

A (2 be / good) _____?

B (3 ✓) _____. There was just
one strange thing.

A (4 what / be / that) _____?

B There was a horrible black cat at the door all day.

A (5 it / be) _____ your
grandma's cat?

B (6 ✗) _____.

**Ⓓ Complete Melanie's message to her friend.
Use *and* or *and then*.**

Yesterday it was sunny (1) _____ we were in the
garden. Suddenly, I was really cold (2) _____
there was a cold hand on my face. There was thunder
(3) _____ there was lightning. But two minutes
later, it was sunny (4) _____ warm again. Is that
strange or what?

2 VOCABULARY

A Read the facts. Circle the correct words.

1 The South Pole has six months of night (no *sun / snow* for 24 hours).

2 The Atacama Desert, Chile is very dry. There is only 0.1 mm of *rain / cloud* every year.

3 Snow and *ice / rain* cover about 10% of the earth.

4 On the 21st of July 1983 in Antarctica, the *temperature / wind* was −89.6°C

5 A *cloud / storm* can weigh more that 500,000 kilos.

6 In 1994, there was a terrible *storm / sun* in the Pacific, for 31 days.

7 *Lightning / Rain* travels at 22,500 km per hour.

8 There is about 0.5 grammes of water in a cubic metre (m³) of *fog / sun.*

B Describe the pictures. Use *cold, warm, hot* and the correct weather words.

Example:

−13°C   20°C

It's very cold and snowy.   1 It's _____ and _____

Its minus thirteen degrees.   It's _____

5°C   30°C

2 It's _____   3 It's _____

_____   _____

−5°C   40°C

4 It's _____   5 It's _____

_____   _____

C Write the four British seasons and the months.

s _____   s _____   a _____   w _____

March   _____   _____   _____

_____   _____   _____   _____

_____   _____   _____   _____

D How do you say the dates? Write them as words.

Example: 2/2 *It's the second of February.*

1 5/12 _____

2 20/7 _____

3 18/9 _____

4 1/4 _____

5 3/11 _____

6 31/3 _____

E Write the correct feelings for the situations.

1 My sister's birthday present was a dog. She was so h_____ !

2 The match was 3–2 to the other team. We were very d_____ .

3 My brother's new girlfriend was at our house yesterday. He was a bit e_____ .

4 There was nothing on TV. I was b_____ .

5 I can't wait for the concert next week. I'm so e_____!

6 On my grandad's last day at work, there was a big party for him. He was very s_____ .

7 One of our friends was in a bad accident last week. We were all very s_____ .

MY WORDS FROM UNIT 5

1 _____

2 _____

3 _____

4 _____

5 _____

After Unit 6:

☐ I know these words. ☺

☐ I don't know these words. ☹ (Learn them again!)

3 COMMUNICATION

25 Ⓐ Circle the correct answer. Then listen and check.

1 What's the weather like?
   A Yes, I like it.   B It's rainy and cold.
   C There isn't any weather today.

2 What's the temperature today?
   A It's about twenty degrees.
   B About 200.
   C It's foggy.

3 It is warm today?
   A Yes, it's minus ten degrees.
   B Yes, there's a strong wind.
   C Yes, it's a really nice day.

4 What was the weather like in your area yesterday?
   A It's sunny.
   B It was sunny.
   C It's a nice area.

5 Do I need a jacket?
   A Yes, it's a bit cold.
   B Yes, it's very dry.
   C I have a jacket, thanks.

26 Ⓑ Complete the story. Write the correct letters
KET (A–H) for 1–5. There are three extra sentences.

It was in the autumn. (1) _____
It was very late. It was nearly midnight.
I wasn't in bed. (2) _____
And I was bored. There was nothing on TV.
Outside it was stormy. (3) _____
Suddenly, there was a loud noise. What was it?
Was it the front door? (4) _____
I was very quiet. And I was very scared.
And then there was another noise. (5) _____
Was I alone? Or was somebody there ...

A It was very near now.
B Was somebody in the house?
C It was warm and sunny.
D It was the 31st of October.
E I have a sister.
F And inside it was cold.
G I was at the sports centre.
H I wasn't tired.

SMART TIP

When you tell a story, describe the time, the place, the weather and your feelings.

4 PRONUNCIATION

27 Ⓐ Listen to the sounds and words. Say the words.

/ɔː/ and /aʊ/
st**or**my   cl**ou**dy

Ⓑ Look at the mouths. Look in a mirror and say the sounds again. Does your mouth look like this?

/ɔː/   /aʊ/

SMART TIP

Look at your mouth in a mirror when you practise pronunciation.

28 Ⓒ Listen to the sounds and words in the box. Put them in the correct list.

| t**ow**er w**a**ll inform**a**tion **ou**tside b**o**red |
| st**o**ry d**ow**n s**ou**nd l**aw**n n**ow** |
| sp**or**t br**ow**n fl**ow**er d**au**ghter |

/ɔː/   /aʊ/

_____   _____

_____   _____

_____   _____

_____   _____

_____   _____

_____   _____

_____   _____

28 Ⓓ Listen and check your answers to exercise C. Then listen again and say the words.

5 CLIL

A Complete the dialogue between two parents with the correct words.

moods	cry	tired	depressed	energy

A Thomas just wants to sleep all the time.

B Maybe he's just (1) _____ from football.

A But he doesn't do sport now. He says he doesn't have the (2) _____

B Maybe he needs to eat more?

A I don't know. He's really sad, too. Almost like he wants to (3) _____ .

B Well, all kids have (4) _____ .
They can't be happy all the time.

A But Thomas is never happy now, and he doesn't see his friends.

B Hmmm. Do you think he's (5) _____ ?

A Maybe. It's more than a bad mood.

B Write sentences about you.

What puts you in a good mood?

I feel in a good mood when _____

_____

_____

_____

What puts you in a bad mood?

_____

_____

_____

_____

6 PORTFOLIO WRITING

A Read Leo's instant message to a friend. Answer the questions with *yes* (Y) or *no* (N).

1 Was it good weather at the weekend? ☐
2 Was Leo at the beach? ☐
3 Was Leo at the skate park? ☐
4 Was he with his friends at the weekend? ☐
5 Was he with his girlfriend? ☐

Hi Ronnie! How's life?
It was fantastic weather here at the weekend.
On Saturday I was in the park with my friends.
But it was too hot for basketball.
On Sunday I was at the beach with my best friend.
How was your weekend?
Were you at home?
Was it good weather?

B In the message, find:

1 a question to ask how somebody is

_____

2 a question to ask about somebody's weekend

_____

C You are Ronnie. Write an answer to Leo's
KET message (40–60 words). Say:

– life is good / bad right now
– where you were at the weekend
– what the weather was like

1 GRAMMAR

Present continuous

We use the present continuous for actions NOW: *I'm doing my homework at the moment.*
We also use it to describe photos: *In this photo, I'm hanging out with my friends at home.*

Positive	Negative
I'**m** (am) he'**s** / she's /it's (**is**)　　　　　　**smiling.** we'**re** / you're / they're (**are**)	I'**m not** (am not) he / she / it **isn't** (is not)　　　　　**smiling.** we / you / they **aren't** (are not)
Questions	Short answers
Am I **Is** he / she / it　　　　　　**smiling?** **Are** you / we / they	Yes, I am. / No, I'm not. Yes, she is. / No, she isn't. Yes, they are. / No, they aren't.

The spelling of the **-ing** form can change:
- ending in one vowel + one consonant:　　sw**im** – sw**imm**ing　s**it** – si**tt**ing
- ending in **-e**　　　　　　　　　　　　　smil**e** – smil**ing**　danc**e** – danc**ing** (**But**: be – being　see – seeing)

A Put in the correct *-ing* form of the words.

run	chat	read	dance	text	cycle

1 They're　　　2 He's　　　3 She's
_____　_____　_____

4 I'm　　　5 We're　　　6 They're
_____　_____　_____

B Complete the message. Use the correct form of the words below.

win	listen	sit	play	write

Hi Seb! I (1) _____ this on Jacob's new phone.

He (2) _____ here in my room. We (3) _____

the new Superfight game. I (4) _____! Ben and Joe

are here too. They (5) _____ to music.

C Complete the sentences. Use negatives.

1　We (not sleep) _____.
　　We're just studying the backs of our eyes.

2　He (not cry) _____.
　　He has something in his eye.

3　I (not tell) _____ lies.
　　I'm being creative with the truth.

4　They (not play) _____ computer games.
　　They're practising their computer skills.

5　She (not feel) _____ ill. She's singing.

D Write the questions. Then match them to the correct answers.

1 What / you / do? _____　☐

　_____

2 you / do / homework? _____　☐

　_____

3 your parents / work? _____　☐

　_____

4 your brother / go / out with Lianne? _____　☐

　_____

a　Yes, he is. Sorry!　　　c　I'm trying!
b　I'm playing a game.　　d　No, they're at home.

2 VOCABULARY

KET A Match the signs (1–5) with five of the gadgets below. There are three extra.

1 At the museum

No 💥 please.
Postcards available in the museum shop.

2 At the cinema   3 In the library

Please turn off during the film.

Please use the 💥 to look for books.

4 In a shop   5 In a hotel

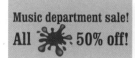

Music department sale! All 💥 50% off!

All rooms with bathroom, phone and 💥

a mobile phones   e games console
b DVD player   f television
c music players   g computers
d cameras   h tablet

SMART TIP

Make notes with the names of things in your home (gadgets, furniture, things in your room). Put the names on the things – and learn them!

KET B Kareem is showing his phone to his grandad. Choose the best word for each space.

I can chat with friends, of course, and
(1) _____ text messages. But I can also
(2) _____ on the internet and (3) _____
email. And I can (4) _____ music videos.
The phone has games – I can (5) _____ games
like this ... There's a camera here, so I can
(6) _____ pictures and videos.

1 A see   B listen to   C send
2 A watch   B go   C type
3 A check   B visit   C text
4 A hear   B look   C watch
5 A do   B play   C like
6 A take   B use   C paint

C Complete the dialogues with the correct words.

screen	app	charger
type	battery	keyboard

1 Do you have your phone?
  – No. The _____ is dead and I can't find
    my _____.

2 Is that your new tablet?
  – Yes. Be careful with the _____!
    Is the _____ easy to use?
  – Yes, you can _____ with all your fingers.

3 This new _____ looks good – it's a football
  game.
  – Can we download it?

D Circle the correct words.

1 I'm playing 🏀 football / basketball.

2 I'm 🎨 painting / drawing.

3 I'm reading a 📖 book / magazine.

4 I'm writing ✏️ an email / in my journal.

5 I'm doing my ✋ hair / nails.

MY WORDS FROM UNIT 6

1 _____
2 _____
3 _____
4 _____
5 _____

After Unit 7:
☐ I know these words. 😊
☐ I don't know these words. 😞 (Learn them again!)

3 COMMUNICATION

29 A Match sentences (a–h) to Jayden or Logan. Write the letters in the boxes. Then listen and check.

1 Jayden likes tech activities.

☐ ☐ ☐ ☐

2 Logan prefers creative, non-tech activities.

☐ ☐ ☐ ☐

a I play the guitar.
b I write ideas and stories in my journal.
c I go on the internet.
d I go on Facebook and I chat with my friends.
e I write my own songs.
f I watch videos on YouTube.
g I play computer games.
h Sometimes I paint or draw.

30 B Two girls are describing their photos. Put their descriptions in the right order to answer the questions. Then listen and check.

1 Who is in the photo?
2 Where are you?
3 What are you doing?
4 What's the weather like?

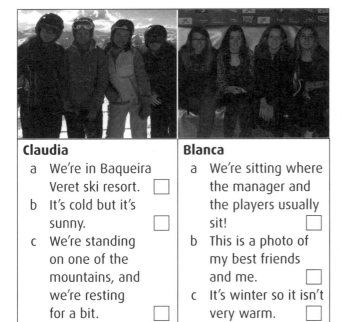

Claudia	Blanca
a We're in Baqueira Veret ski resort. ☐	a We're sitting where the manager and the players usually sit! ☐
b It's cold but it's sunny. ☐	b This is a photo of my best friends and me. ☐
c We're standing on one of the mountains, and we're resting for a bit. ☐	c It's winter so it isn't very warm. ☐
d In this photo, you can see me and my friends. ☐	d We're at the stadium of Español FC. ☐

4 PRONUNCIATION

31 A Listen to the sounds and words. Then listen again and repeat.

/tʃ/   /dʒ/
wat**ch**   ga**dg**et

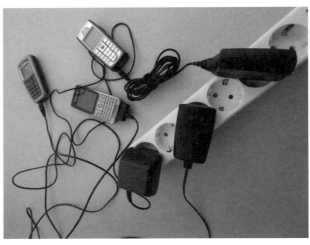

32 B Listen to the sentences. Look at the words in bold.

– **Mark the /tʃ/ sound with a red pen.**
– **Mark the /dʒ/ sound with a blue pen.**
– **Which TWO words have both sounds? Circle them.**

1 She's **checking** her **charger**.
2 They're chatting about **technology**.
3 He's **changing** his **jeans**.
4 We're **watching** a band on **stage**.
5 He's writing a **message** in his **journal**.
6 She's **choosing** a new **jacket**.

32 C Listen again to the sentences in exercise B and repeat.

33 D Listen to these sentences and repeat. Then listen again and say the words fast!

check	chat	change
journal	jacket	jeans

5 CLIL

A **Write the words for the definitions.**

1 Films with moving pictures or models.

an _____

2 A person or animal in a film or series.

ch _____

3 Pictures that show a story.

st _____

4 A small copy of a person or thing.

m _____

5 When you make something flat.

sq _____

6 When you make something thin.

st _____

SMART TIP

Write and learn words with their English definitions.

B **Read about Shunichi's favourite animation series. Then write four or five sentences about your favourite animation series.**

My favourite animation series, by Shunichi

My favourite animation series is *Naruto*. It's a Japanese series. Naruto is a teenager with a terrible monster in him. The people in his village hate him. But Naruto is very brave and he can do martial arts. He fights a lot and usually wins.

My favourite animation series, by _____

_____

_____

_____

_____

_____

_____

6 PORTFOLIO WRITING

A **Read Rex's and Grecia's status on their social media pages. What are they doing now? Tick (✓) the activities.**

1 having lunch ☐
2 listening to music ☐
3 learning to drive ☐
4 taking a test ☐
5 hanging out with friends ☐
6 saying English words ☐

Rex

Life is good! OK day at school today. Pizza for lunch and not too much homework ☺. Now I'm surfing the net for information about teenage drivers (I'm writing an article for the school magazine). I'm listening to Blu – love his lyrics.

Grecia

5 out of 20 in my English test. ☹ My teacher wasn't happy! And my parents say I can't see my friends this evening – I need to learn vocabulary. So now I'm listening to a DVD with English words and I'm repeating them. Life is hard.

B **In the status sentences, find the phrases with these meanings:**

1 I'm feeling happy with everything.

_____

2 I'm not very happy now.

_____

C **Write your status for today (30–50 words).**
KET **Write about:**

– how school was today
– what you're doing now
– how you're feeling

1 GRAMMAR

A Complete this story about the Winchester Mystery House in California, USA. Use the correct form of *was* or *were*.

One day in the 1970s, a tour guide and some visitors (1) _____ in a kitchen in the Winchester Mystery House. There (2) _____ a nice smell of warm chicken soup. But there (3) _____ any soup. The last cooking in this kitchen (4) _____ in the 1920s. A few months later, a different tour guide (5) _____ in the same kitchen with a group – they (6) _____ the same visitors as before but different visitors. There (7) _____ the smell of chicken soup again. All the people in the group (8) _____ sure about this.

B Now complete this story with *and / and then*.

I was in the Winchester Mystery House on a tour. There was an old man in old black clothes (1) _____ a black hat next to me. He was very still (2) _____ quiet. (3) _____ suddenly he wasn't there. It was very strange. We were in another room later (4) _____ suddenly there was another old man next me. It wasn't the same man, but his clothes (5) _____ his hat were exactly the same.

C Write the dialogue. Use the correct form of the present continuous.

Dad (1) What / you / do?

_____

Cody (2) I / look / at a website about ghosts.

_____

Dad (3) Why / you / look / at that?

_____

Cody (4) We / do / a project on ghosts at school.

_____

(5) I / not read / it for fun!

Dad (6) everybody in your class / do / the same project?

_____

Cody (7) Yes, but we / not work / together.

_____

(8) Every student / find / different information.

_____

2 VOCABULARY

A Complete the information with the correct words from the box.

sunny dry sun wet rain

In the UK, there are about 1,360 hours of (1) _____ a year. That means it's (2) _____ for about three and a half hours every day. There is about 1,150 mm of (3) _____ every year. But in 1965, it was very (4) _____ (only 120 mm), and in 1995, it was very (5) _____ (480).

winter cold summer degrees hot temperature

The average (6) _____ for the whole year is 8.5 (7) _____. The UK has cool winters and warm summers. In the (8) _____ , it is about 14 degrees and in the (9) _____ it is 3.5 degrees. But on 30 December 1991 in Braemar, Scotland, it was very (10) _____ (-27.2 degrees). In Faversham, England, it was very (11) _____ on 10 August 2003 (38.5 degrees).

B What gadget is it?

1 It has a battery. You can take pictures with it.

_____

2 It has a screen. You can watch films, your favourite series and other programmes on it.

_____

3 You use this with a TV to watch films and music videos.

_____

4 You can listen to music anywhere with this. But you can't chat to friends.

_____

5 You can send text messages with it and download apps.

6 It has a big keyboard and you usually use it at a desk. You can do school projects on it.

_____

7 It's like a big flat screen. You can do everything on it!

_____

8 You can play games with this on a TV or other screen.

_____

C Complete the words for feelings with a, e, i or u.

1 When I feel s__d or d__s__pp__ __nte__, I play my guitar.
2 When I feel h__ppy or __xc__t__d, I draw and paint.
3 When I feel b__r__d, I read magazines.
4 When I feel sc__r__d or __mb__rr__ss__d, I write in my journal.

3 LISTENING (KET)

36 ▶ **Listen to Ruby talking to Luca about free time activities.**

For questions 1-6, choose A, B or C.

1 Ruby's visitor is …
   A her aunt.
   B a female cousin.
   C a male cousin.
2 Football isn't a good idea because …
   A there's nowhere to play.
   B her cousin can't play it.
   C Ruby can't play it.
3 Ruby doesn't want to go swimming because
   A she hates it.
   B she can't swim.
   C it's too cold.
4 Ruby and her cousin can't play video games because …
   A she doesn't have a games console.
   B she doesn't like video games.
   C her cousin doesn't like video games.
5 At the film festival, you can watch films …
   A from 8 am to 8 pm.
   B from 2 pm to 2 am.
   C from 8 am to 2 am.
6 Tickets for films are …
   A £3.
   B £10.
   C £13.

4 READING (KET)

Read the story about the Winchester Mystery House. Choose the best word (A, B or C) for each space.

The Winchester Mystery House is a strange house. It has 160 rooms, two thousand doors, thirteen bathrooms (1) _____ six kitchens. In the house, (2) _____ are doors and windows onto walls. There are corridors with walls at the end. And there are stairs (3) _____ nowhere!

The house was the house (4) _____ Sarah Winchester. The Winchester family was the maker of the (5) _____ Winchester rifles (a kind of gun), and they were very rich. A lot of people were (6) _____ because of Winchester rifles. After the deaths of her daughter and husband, Sarah was (7) _____ because the ghosts of these people were in (8) _____ house. The many rooms were a way to get away from the ghosts.

1 A and   B and then   C because
2 A it   B they   C there
3 A past   B to   C along
4 A of   B from   C by
5 A famous   B safe   C healthy
6 A friendly B tired   C dead
7 A scared   B surprised   C excited
8 A their   B her   C his

1 GRAMMAR

Comparatives and superlatives

We use **comparative adjectives** (and *than*) to compare two things or people.
*I'm **older than** Luiz.*   *My feet are **bigger than** my dad's feet.*
We add *-er* to short adjectives (all one-syllable adjectives, some two-syllable adjectives):
cheap – cheaper
We use *more* with long adjectives (some two-syllable adjectives, all adjectives with three or more syllables):
expensive – more expensive

We use **superlative adjectives** to compare things or people in a group.
*I'm **the oldest** in my class.*   *I have **the biggest** feet in my family.*
We use *the* and *-est* with short adjectives: *cheap – the cheapest*
We use *the most* with long adjectives: *expensive – the most expensive*
Good and *bad* have irregular forms.

Adjective	Comparative	Superlative
Short adjectives		
cheap	cheap**er**	**the** cheap**est**
Long adjectives		
expensive	**more** expensive	**the most** expensive
Irregular adjectives		
good	better	**the best**
bad	worse	**the worst**

The spelling of the *-er* and *-est* forms can change:
- adjectives ending in **-e**
  nic**e** – nic**er**– nic**est**
- adjectives ending in one vowel*
  + one consonant:
  b**ig** – b**igg**er –b**igg**est
- adjectives ending in *-y*
  happ**y** – happ**ier** –happ**iest**

*not two vowels

A Write the correct comparative and superlative forms of these adjectives in your notebook.

| international | good | ugly |
| creative | hot | cool |

Adjective	Comparative	Superlative

B Now complete the sentences with the correct forms of the words from A.

1 I always wear the same style. My sister is _____ than me with clothes.
2 My school shoes are horrible. They're much _____ than my normal shoes.
3 That shoe shop is the _____ shoe shop in this town. The shoes are great and they aren't expensive.
4 It's _____ fashion show in the world. There are clothes from lots of different countries.
5 It's _____ today than yesterday. Just wear shorts.
6 Everyone is wearing those jeans. They're _____ brand right now.

C Look at the table and compare the students. Use the correct comparative or superlative form of *tall, small, heavy, good or confident*.

Aziz	Lin	Maria
170 cm	162 cm	164 cm
55 kg	45 kg	60 kg
Good health	Very good health	Not good health
Not confident	Very confident	Confident

1 Aziz is the _____ person.
2 Maria is 164 cm. She's _____ than Aziz.
3 Aziz is _____ than Lin, but Maria is the _____ person.
4 Maria has the _____ health.
5 Maria is _____ than Aziz, but Lin is the _____ person.

SMART TIP

Learn the three forms (adjective, comparative, superlative) together. For adjectives with two syllables, check the forms in a dictionary.

2 VOCABULARY

A Complete the dialogues with the correct money words.

Girl Dad, can I have a bigger (1) a_____?

Dad No, you can't. Why don't you (2) s_____ less money – and try and (3) s_____ something. Or get a job and (4) e_____ some money.

Boy On this website, the phone (5) c_____ 80 euros. How much is that in pounds?

Girl Use this website. You can change (6) p_____ into a different (7) c_____ ... Look.

Boy Cool. So I have enough money for that! I can buy it and give my old phone to (8) c_____.

B Complete the crossword with the correct clothes words.

ACROSS →

1 You wear it on your head.
5 A sort of T-shirt for girls.
7 Sports shoes.
8 It keeps the top part of your body warm.
9 Winter shoes.   10 Summer shoes.

DOWN ↓

1 This covers the top part of your body and your head.
2 You wear it over other clothes.
3 Short trousers.
4 You wear them when it's sunny.
6 You wear it round your neck.
9 Your jeans don't fall down with this.

SMART TIP

Find a crossword maker online. Write in words and explanations. Make your crossword and give it to a partner.

C Complete the sentences with the correct opposite adjective.

1 Our football shorts are dark blue and our T-shirts are _____ blue.
2 These boots are so uncomfortable. They just aren't _____ at all.
3 This jacket wasn't expensive, it was quite _____.
4 I don't like tight jeans. I prefer _____ trousers.
5 We can't wear _____ skirts at school, only long skirts.
6 This coat isn't _____, it's quite old-fashioned – but I love it!

KET D Match the signs (1-6) to the correct descriptions (A-H). There are two extra.

 1   2   3

 4   5   GARAGE SALE Saturday 8am 6

A Always wear safety equipment in the factory.
B Please do not shop here.
C Dangerous chemicals!
D We have all kinds of old stuff.
E Please put your rubbish in the bin.
F Danger! Falling trees.
G Please recycle.
H Don't pollute the water!

MY WORDS FROM UNIT 7

1 _____
2 _____
3 _____
4 _____
5 _____

After Unit 8:
☐ I know these words. ☺
☐ I don't know these words. ☹ (Learn them again!)

3 COMMUNICATION

37 Ⓐ **Put the conversations in the correct order. Write 1, 2, 3, 4 in the boxes. Then listen and check.**

1 a How much are these jeans? ☐
   b Yes, can I help you? ☐
   c Excuse me. ☐
   d I think they're £50. Let me check. ☐

2 a Yes, of course. ☐
   b Erm, where's the changing room? ☐
   c Can I try these on? ☐
   d Oh sorry, it's over there. ☐

3 a OK. Do you have it in small? ☐
   b No, sorry, only in brown. ☐
   c Small? Yes, ... here you are. ☐
   d Do you have this jacket in black? ☐

38 Ⓑ **Choose the correct answer for the questions. Then listen and check.**

1 Do you like those trainers?
   A Yes, but they're the most expensive in the shop!
   B Yes, but they're the worst in the shop!

2 Is your mum older than your dad?
   A Yes, she's 40 and he's 45.
   B Yes, he's 40 and she's 45.

3 Is this the smallest size you have?
   A No, I think we have a smaller size.
   B No, I think we have a bigger size.

4 Are you the tallest in your family?
   A Yes, my brother's taller than me.
   B No, I'm the shortest.

5 Are they your favourite boots?
   A Yes, they're the most uncomfortable boots ever, but they look great!
   B Yes, they're the ugliest and most uncomfortable boots ever!

4 PRONUNCIATION

39 Ⓐ **Listen to the sentence. Can you say it? How many /st/ sounds can you hear? Listen again and check.**

39 Ⓑ **Listen to the /st/ sound at the <u>beginning</u> of the words in the box and repeat.**

| style | stuff | story | statement | student |
| star | stand | start | stop | stage |

39 Ⓒ **Listen to the /st/ sound at the <u>end</u> of these words and repeat.**

| cost | interest | best | trendiest | artist | last |
| easiest | smallest | worst | fastest |

39 Ⓓ **Now add an /r/ to the /st/ at the beginning: /str/. Listen and repeat these words.**

| strong | street | strict | strange |
| straight | stretch |

Ⓔ **Write your own sentence. Use words from B, C and D. Then read it out. Is it easy to say?**

_____

_____

_____

5 CLIL

A Circle the correct words.

Many people get (1) *scam websites / scam emails* from strangers. Usually the stranger asks you for help: he / she knows about millions of dollars in a (2) *bank account / statement.* You can get some of the money! The stranger then asks you for your bank account information: a (3) *balance / credit card* number or the (4) *password / interest* to your online bank account. But when you get your (5) *statement / credit card* or check your (6) *balance / pin number,* you get a big shock. Your money isn't there. It was a scam!

B Read about Lola's bank account. Then write about your bank account. (Or ask your parents and write about their account.)

My bank account *by Lola*

I have a bank account with Santander Bank in Madrid. It's a savings account and I get 3% interest. I have a debit card for my account but I don't use it very often. I usually save my money. I use my bank account online because it's easier. I get online statements every month. I'm very careful with my bank information.

My bank account, by _____

_____

_____

_____

_____

_____

6 PORTFOLIO WRITING

A Read Dylan's online adverts for some old stuff. Complete the information for each advert.

Item	Bike	Guitar
Description		
Age		
Condition		
Price		

For sale: Bike   Price: £30

Boy's bike, black and red with 10 gears.
Five years old and in quite good condition.

Ask for more information!

For sale: Electric guitar Price: £120

Red and white electric guitar. Great sound.

You can use it with a computer and USB.

Two years old and in very good condition.

For sale because I don't play now.

B Complete the phrases from the adverts with the correct prepositions.

1 _____ sale.
2 It's _____ quite good / very good condition.
3 Ask _____ more information.

C Write one or two online adverts for your old **KET** stuff.

  – Describe the item.
  – Write its age and condition.
  – Give a price.

1 GRAMMAR

Past simple

We use the past simple to talk about completed actions in the past.

For the past simple form of regular verbs, we add -ed to the verb: ask – ask**ed**

- verbs ending in **–e**:   smile – smile**d**
- verbs ending in one vowel + one consonant: drop – dro**pped**
- verbs ending in consonant + -y: try – tr**ied**

Irregular verbs have different forms. Examples: see – *saw* go – *went*

To make negatives and questions (regular and irregular verbs), we use *did* + verb.

Positive		Negative	
I / we / you / they he / she / it	watch**ed** TV.	I / we / you / they he / she / it	**didn't (did not)** watch TV.
Questions		Short answers	
Did I / you / we / they he / she / it	watch TV?	Yes, I **did**. No, I **didn't**.	

We often use these time phrases with the past simple:

this morning / this afternoon / yesterday / last week / last month / last year / last summer / two years ago / in 2010

A Complete the email with the correct past simple form.

Quick links | Search mail

Hi Mom and Dad

Everything is OK at camp. Yesterday we (1 *go*) _____ on a hiking trip. We (2 *walk*) _____ 25 km in the mountains. I really (3 *enjoy*) _____ it. We (4 *see*) _____ lots of animals and I (5 *take*) _____ lots of photos.

I was very tired this morning, I just (6 *want*) _____ to stay in bed! But we (7 *have*) _____ breakfast and (8 *play*) _____ tennis and then I was OK. This afternoon I (9 *try*) _____ one of the power boats for the first time and then we (10 *swim*) _____ in the lake. Awesome!

Love

Catalina

SMART TIP

When you learn a new verb, learn its past simple form too.

B Nicolae went to New York on holiday. Write the words in the questions in the right order.

1 did / you / get back / when ?
2 how long / stay / there / did / you ?
3 go up / you / the Empire State Building / did ?
4 there / what else / see / you / did ?
5 a lot of shopping / do / you / did ?
6 like / did / New York / you ?

C Complete Nicolae's answers.

a We (visit) _____ the Statue of Liberty but we (not climb) _____ up it.
b Yesterday morning, I (feel) _____ really tired all day.
c I (love) _____ it! We just (not have) _____ enough time there.
d No, we _____. I (not want) _____ to buy anything.
e Yes, we _____. But we (not see) _____ much because it was rainy.
f We (not stay) _____ there long – only one week.

D Match the questions and answers in exercises B and C.

2 VOCABULARY

A Complete the countries with *a, e, i, o, u*. Then write the correct continent: *Europe, North America or Asia*.

Country	Continent
1 Fr_nc_	_____
2 _S_	_____
3 Sp__n	_____
4 Ch_n_	_____
5 _t_ly	_____
6 _n_t_d K_ngd_m	_____
7 T_rk_y	_____
8 G_rm_ny	_____
9 M_l_ys__	_____
10 M_x_c_	_____

B Write the correct places to stay.

1 h_____ 2 t_____ 3 h_____ 4 c_____

5 g____h____ 6 h____a____ 7 c_____ 8 m_____

C Complete the students' sentences about holidays with the correct places.

island	mountains	countryside	rainforest
sea	field	lake	forest

1 We always go on holiday to the _____. We love the beach.
2 This year, we want to stay on an _____ in the South Pacific.
3 We usually stay in a little house in the _____, with trees all round.
4 My family always goes camping in a farmer's _____.
5 We live in the city, so we like to spend our holidays in the _____.
6 I'd like to visit the _____ and see all the animals there.
7 In winter, we usually go skiing in the _____.
8 On holiday, we have a boat and we go out on the _____ every day.

D Match the adverts to the correct words.

a) ancient monument   b) theme park
c) seaside resort   d) cruise   e) castle

1 Spend your holiday in Side in Turkey. There are lots of hotels, restaurants and shops here – and a great beach.

2 Enjoy a day out at Tivoli in Copenhagen, Denmark. Go on rides, listen to concerts and eat in the cafés and restaurants.

3 Travel down the beautiful Danube River and visit Vienna, Budapest and Bratislava on our luxury boats.

4 Visit Athens' most famous building. Pericles built the Parthenon in the fifth century BC, and it is still one of the most beautiful buildings in the world.

5 Come to Neuschwanstein in Bavaria, one of Germany's most popular tourist attractions. You can visit King Ludwig II's rooms on the third and fourth floors.

E Now choose the correct preposition in these adverts.

1 No time for a holiday? Go *to / on* a day trip!
2 It's easy to get here *in / by* plane from most big cities.
3 Bored? Why not go *to / at* a theme park?
4 Stay *in / on* one of our luxury holiday apartments.
5 A bed *at / by* our hostel costs only $20 a night!
6 Want to stay fit? Go hiking *on / in* the mountains.

MY WORDS FROM UNIT 8

1 _____
2 _____
3 _____
4 _____
5 _____

After Unit 9:

☐ I know these words. ☺
☐ I don't know these words. ☹ (Learn them again!)

3 COMMUNICATION

40 Ⓐ **Diana is telling the class about her last holiday. Complete what she says. Write the correct letters (A–H) for 1–5. There are three extra. Then listen and check.**

KET

> In my last holidays, I went on holiday to Italy.
>
> (1) I went with _____
>
> We were in a little town by the sea.
>
> (2) We had _____
>
> We were in the water a lot.
>
> (3) We went _____
>
> We usually ate in the apartment but sometimes we went to restaurants.
>
> (4) The food was _____
>
> At home, Italian food is always pizza and pasta.
>
> (5) But on holiday we tried _____

A   really good.
B   tennis lessons.
C   a holiday apartment there.
D   photos of the mountains.
E   lots of other things.
F   my parents and my sister.
G   a terrible time.
H   swimming and water skiing.

40 Ⓑ **Read the start of the conversation. Put the rest of the conversation in the correct order. Write 1-8 in the boxes.**

> Something really embarrassing happened to me yesterday. –

> OK ... Where were you?

a   You what? You asked her out? ☐
b   Well, I went bright red. And then I asked her out. ☐
c   So what happened?
d   At my cousin's party. ☐
e   Yeah. And she said yes! ☐
f   Wow, I need to try that! ☐
g   Mmm, a bit embarrassing. What did you do then? ☐
h   I fell over somebody's leg and then I fell on this really pretty girl. ☐

4 PRONUNCIATION

41 Ⓐ **Listen to the sounds and words. Say the words.**

/ɪ/	/iː/
Italy	Sw**e**den
tour**i**st	**e**cotourism

41 Ⓑ **Listen to the words in the box. Put them in the correct list.**

> b**ri**lliant   s**ea**   pr**i**son   **E**nglish   f**ie**ld
> tr**i**p   th**e**me park   t**e**nnis   b**ea**ch   **ea**t
> dolph**i**n   h**i**ll   sn**ee**ze   Pac**i**fic
> sight**see**ing   sl**ee**p

/ɪ/	/iː/
_____	_____
_____	_____
_____	_____
_____	_____
_____	_____
_____	_____
_____	_____
_____	_____

41 Ⓒ **Listen and check. Then listen again and say the words.**

SMART TIP

Record yourself when you repeat words. Then listen to the recording and check your own pronunciation.

5 CLIL

KET **A** Read the text. Choose the best word for each space.

Samoa is a group of ten islands in (1) _____ between New Zealand and Hawaii. Its rainforests, beaches, fish and animals make Samoa a popular place for (2) _____ holidays. Tourists stay in beach *fale*, (3) _____ houses with no walls by the sea.

In the sea around Samoa, you can see (4) _____ . And near one island, you can swim with huge green (5) _____ in their natural (6) _____. The local people look after them and (7) _____ them from . (8) _____ .

1	A Africa	B North America	C the Pacific Ocean
2	A safari	B ecotourism	C snowboarding
3	A simple	B luxury	C modern
4	A birds	B dolphins	C iguanas
5	A crocodiles	B frogs	C turtles
6	A habitat	B park	C place
7	A kill	B protect	C eat
8	A tourists	B guards	C hunters

B Write about a protected area in your country. Use the questions to help you.

Where is the area?
What is the area like?
Why is it a protected area?
What animals can you see?
What other activities can you do?
Where can you stay?

_____
_____
_____
_____
_____
_____

6 PORTFOLIO WRITING

A Lucy is planning a camping trip with her dad and two friends. Read her text message to her friends. Which things should her friends bring? Circle the letters.

For our camping trip at the weekend, remember to bring:
> your tent
> a sleeping bag and a mat
> a torch (it gets really dark at night!)

You also need:
> walking boots
> a good jacket

And don't forget:
> lunch for Saturday
> a water bottle

See you at my house on Saturday at 9.00.
Don't be late!

B Find the phrases in the text message with these meanings:

1 Please bring.

_____

2 Come at the right time.

_____

C You're planning a hiking trip with your friends
KET for one day. Write a text message to them (40–60 words). Tell them what to bring. Decide what **YOU** think is important. Think about:

– equipment
– food
– clothes

1 GRAMMAR

A Matt is comparing three hotels. Complete his sentences. Use the correct form of the words in the box to compare the hotels.

family-friendly	small	good	near
expensive	big	cheap	

Hotel Golden Beach
★★★★
hotel (120 rooms)

50 metres to beach

Good food

Family price: £770

Family rating:
☺☺☺

Hotel Tropicana
★★★
hotel (34 rooms)

1.5 km to beach

Good food

Family price: £495

Family rating:
☺☺☺☺☺

Hotel Paradise
★★★★
hotel (500 rooms)

200 metres to beach

Fantastic food

Family price: £650

Family rating:
☺☺☺☺

1 Hotel Golden Beach is _____ to the beach.
2 But it's _____.
3 Hotel Tropicana is _____ than the other two hotels – only 34 rooms.
4 But it's _____ and _____ than the others.
5 Hotel Paradise is _____ hotel.
6 The food there is _____ than the other two hotels.

B Complete the message. Use the correct past simple form of the verbs.

Hi Ginny

We (1 *arrive*) _____ here OK yesterday evening. Today we (2 *go*) _____ shopping in a really big supermarket. They (3 *have*) _____ everything! Mum and Dad (4 *love*) _____ it. We (5 *get*) _____ lots of food and I (6 *try*) _____ on some sandals. This afternoon we (7 *stay*) _____ by the pool at the apartment. I (8 *read*) _____ the guide book and (9 *look*) _____ for some places to visit. Then I (10 *swim*) _____ in the pool. It's great here!

Rachel

C Complete the dialogue.

A (1 you / enjoy) _____ the trip?
B Yes, but we (2 not see) _____ everything. We (3 not have) _____ enough time.
A (4 you have) _____ lunch?
B Yes, but just a salad. We (5 not want) _____ a big meal. What about you? What (6 you / do) _____? (7 you / go) _____ to the village?
A No, we (8 not leave) _____ the hotel. We were too tired.

2 VOCABULARY

A Read some definitions of money words. Write the correct word for each one.

1 You get this money every month from your parents.
  a_____
2 What you pay for something.
  p_____
3 This organisation helps people.
  c_____
4 It's the type of money in different countries.
  c_____
5 You do this when have money but don't use it.
  s_____
6 You do this when you buy something.
  s_____
7 You do this when you work for money.
  e_____
8 How much money something is.
  c_____

B **Write what the students are wearing.**

1 She's wearing a tight _____ with a _____, white _____ and _____ .

2 He's wearing a long _____ , _____ and trendy _____ .

3 She's wearing a _____ , a _____ , a short _____ and _____ .

4 She's wearing a baggy _____ , _____ and comfortable _____ .

C **In the word search (→ ↓ ↘), find eight words each for:**

places to stay	places

```
J J Y L F D A P A R T M E N T
C W P K K T F K L X B M C P G
A T N N J G V I T T R T A F I
M Q E M M R C R E G K F R F S
P P Y N R O H W V L L J A X L
S N R L T A U H L N D L V H A
I Z C N S V I N O N F L A O N
T N Z M E B V N T S M N N T D
E J Q M A T C X F A T G J E L
R F O R E S T J N O I E N L C
X X P L V D N X T K R N L D M
C O U N T R Y S I D E E S N M
F G U E S T H O U S E L S M M
M O T E L J B V J T G B L T T
```

3 LISTENING KET

42 Listen to a conversation in a clothes shop. Complete questions 1–5.

Order form		
Clothes item	1	_____
Colour	2	_____
Price	3	_____
Size	4	_____
Customer name and phone number	5	Julia Flowers _____

4 READING KET

Complete the postcard. Write one word for each space.

Hi Thomas

Hello (1) ____ Crete! I'm sitting (2) _____ a café at the moment and I'm (3) _____ at the sea. We're staying in (4) _____ lovely hotel in a small seaside resort. It's really pretty (5) _____ the hotel has a great swimming pool. Yesterday, we (6) _____ hiking in the Samaria Gorge. We got (7) _____ early and took the bus there and then (8) ____ walked 16 kilometres. It was a long walk and it (9) _____ very hot, but I really enjoyed it.

See (10) _____ soon!

Love Rosie

Unit 9 ▓▓ Loves & hates

1 GRAMMAR

Like + gerund or infinitive

After *like / love / hate / prefer,* we can use two forms:

to + verb (infinitive)   OR   **verb + -ing** (gerund)
*I like **to watch** TV.*   *I like **watching** TV.*

Remember the spelling of the *-ing* form can change.
- ending in one vowel + one consonant   sw**im** – *swimming*   h**it** – *hitting*
- ending in **-e**   rid**e** – *riding*   skat**e** – *skating*
                                                              (**But**: be – *being*   see – *seeing*)

A Complete the information using the correct verbs from the box.

> getting   giving   going   wearing
> collecting   looking

I love (1) _____ things with bows – bags and things for my hair. And I like (2) _____ clothes with bows! I love (3) _____ to markets to find new things. I also like (4) _____ in shops at the mall. I love (5) _____ something new for my collection! I never swap things – I hate (6) _____ anything away.

B Write the dialogues. Use gerunds.

Example: A   you / like
              Do you like dancing?
          B   (✓) Yes, I do.

1   A   you / like

    B   (✗) _____

2   A   you / like

    B   (✓) _____

3   A   you / like

    B   (✓) _____

4   A   you / like

    B   (✗) _____

C Complete the email. Write one word for each space.

Quick links | Search mail

Hi Sunisa

You asked about what I like and don't like. Well, I love (1) _____ gymnastics, but I don't like (2) _____ football or any other ball sports. Sometimes I like (3) _____ films at home, but I prefer (4) _____ to the cinema. At the weekend, I like (5) _____ out with my friends at home – but I hate (6) _____ up early for school on Mondays!

What about you?

Anna

D Complete Sunisa's reply to Anna's email in C. Use *and* or *but*.

Quick links | Search mail

Hi Anna

I hate gymnastics, (1)_____ I love football! I like playing volleyball (2) _____ I like playing tennis too. At the weekend, I meet my friends (3) _____ I also like doing things on my own. I love taking photos (4) _____ making videos. I also collect old film posters, (5) _____ I don't have very many.

Write soon

Sunisa

44

2 VOCABULARY

A **Read the sentences. Then combine *make* or *collect* with a word from the box and write each person's hobby.**

> model planes   cakes   football cards
> coins   videos   postcards   stamps

Example: I *collect postcards*. I have a lot with funny pictures of animals.

1 I _____. Sometimes I put them on YouTube.

2 I _____. I just like building them, they don't fly.

3 I _____. I don't buy them at the post office, I get them on the internet.

4 I _____. My friend and I make fantasy teams with the players.

5 I _____. I have euros from lots of different countries.

6 I _____. I sell them at school to get money for charity.

SMART TIP

Remember: When you learn a word, learn its collocations.

B **Read the definitions and write the names of the sports.**

1 You do this on a bike.
   c_____

2 You play it with a small plastic ball.
   t_____ t_____

3 You do it on a horse.
   r_____

4 You do running, jumping and throwing.
   a_____

5 You hit a ball and then run round four bases.
   b_____

6 You do tricks on a board at a skate park.
   s_____

7 You play it on grass with a ball and a stick.
   h_____

8 You hit a ball with your hands or arms.
   v_____

9 You move your body in lots of strange ways.
   g_____

10 You do it on ice.
   i_____-s_____

C **Complete the dialogues with the correct form of *play*, *go* or *do*.**

1 Do you want to _____ table tennis?
   – Yeah, great.

2 Where's Mum? – She's _____ gymnastics.

3 Do you like athletics?
   – I like watching it on TV but I don't like _____ it.

4 Do you _____ football at school?
   – Yes, and I play in a club too.

5 What sports do you do?
   – In winter I often _____ ice-skating.

6 What did you do at the weekend?
   – We _____ cycling.

D **Look at the pictures. Write complete sentences with the names of the missing equipment.**

1 He doesn't have a _____   2 She_____

3_____   4 _____

5 _____   6 _____

MY WORDS FROM UNIT 9

1 _____

2 _____

3 _____

4 _____

5 _____

After Unit 10:

☐ I know these words. ☺

☐ I don't know these words. ☹ (Learn them again!)

3 COMMUNICATION

43 ⓐ Match the questions and answers. Then listen and check.

1 What's your favourite sport?
  A No, I don't.   B I love swimming.
  C Yes, it's my favourite.

2 Are you in a team or club?
  A I'm a member of the tennis club.   B I don't know.
  C Our school team never wins.

3 Do you support a team or club?
  A I don't like playing football.
  B No, they don't support me.   C No, I don't.

4 Do you watch sport?
  A I sometimes go to volleyball matches.
  B We took first place in the championship.
  C It starts at 3 o'clock.

5 Why do you like this sport?
  A It's unhealthy.   B It's so boring.   C I'm good at it.

44 ⓑ Put the conversations in the right order. Write 1, 2, 3, 4 in the boxes. Then listen and check.

1 a Yes, I do, especially films. What about you? ☐
  b I prefer listening to music. ☐
  c Do you like watching TV? ☐
  d I like listening to music too. ☐

2 a Oh no, I hate cooking. ☐
  b I hate tidying my room. ☐
  c Mmm, sometimes I quite like cooking. ☐
  d Me too! I hate doing stuff in the house. ☐

3 a It's easy, you should try it! ☐
  b What sports do you like? ☐
  c Really? I can't ski. ☐
  d I love skiing. ☐

4 PRONUNCIATION

45 ⓐ Look at the questions and answers. In the answers, the stress is on the two different ideas. Listen to the conversations. Then listen again and repeat.

A Do you play football and hockey?
B I don't play <u>football</u>, but I play <u>hockey</u>.

A Do you like skiing and water skiing?
B I like <u>skiing</u>, but I don't like <u>water skiing</u>.

46 ⓑ Listen and underline the stress in these sentences. Then listen again and repeat.

1 You don't play tennis with a bat; you play it with a racket.
2 I don't collect stamps; I collect coins.
3 He isn't in the basketball team; he's in the baseball team.
4 She isn't a snowboarder; she's a skateboarder.
5 I don't make model planes; I make model boats.
6 We don't play football; we watch it.

ⓒ Write two sentences about you with two different ideas. Use the sentences in A and B to help you. Then read them out with the correct stress.

5 CLIL

KET **A** Read the text and choose the best word for each space.

My friend's brother has a phobia about dogs. He tries to (1) _____ them and he does exercises to (2) _____ when he sees a dog.

I hate speaking in front of lots of people. I'm so scared I feel (3) _____ and I can't (4) _____. Mum says it's a (5) _____ phobia.

Our neighbour has agoraphobia. She's (6) _____ to go out. She takes (7) _____ for it. And she's getting help to (8) _____ her phobia.

1	A love	B hate	C avoid
2	A relax	B get fit	C be healthy
3	A happy	B sick	C excited
4	A go out	B walk	C breathe
5	A social	B specific	C public
6	A embarrassed	B afraid	C surprised
7	A water	B medicine	C help
8	A enjoy	B face	C save

B Write about things you hate or hate doing. Use these phrases:

I really don't like ...   I hate ...
I'm afraid of ...   ... makes me feel sick.
I always avoid ...

_____

_____

_____

_____

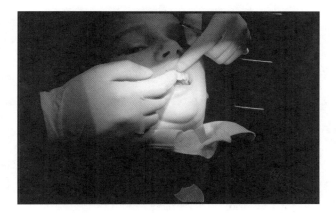

6 PORTFOLIO WRITING

A Read Ben's message and complete the ticket.

Hi Ali and Roman

Would you like to come to a football match with me on 15th October? Manchester United versus Liverpool at Old Trafford! Dad just got four tickets. Kick off is at 12.45. Let me know!

TICKET
Match: _____ versus _____
At: _____
Date: _____
Kick off time: _____

B Now read Roman's and Ali's replies. Complete the sentence below.

Ali Fantastic, thanks a lot. I'll be there! Hope Man United wins!

Roman I'm sorry but I can't come. It's my dad's 40th birthday party that day. Thanks anyway!

_____ can't come because _____

C Look at the three messages in A and B again. Underline the phrases with these meanings:

1 to invite somebody to something
2 to ask for an answer
3 to say you'll come
4 to say you can't come
5 to thank somebody when you say no

D Now look at these phrases and match them to three phrases in exercise C.

a I'd love to come.
b I'd like to invite you to ...
c I'm afraid I can't come.

E Write an instant message and invite a friend to
KET a sports event (40-60 words). Write:

– what event it is and the date
– where it is
– what time it starts

1 GRAMMAR

Adverbs of manner and frequency

Adverbs of manner describe HOW we do something.

*He eats **noisily**.   She cooks really **well**.*

To make these adverbs, we usually add *-ly* to the adjective.

> safe – *safely*   bad – *badly*

But the spelling sometimes changes:

> adjectives ending in *y*:
> happy – *happily*   easy – *easily*

> adjectives ending in consonant + *le*:
> horrib**le** – *horribly*

Some adverbs are irregular:

> hard – *hard*   fast – *fast*   good – *well*

Adverbs of frequency describe HOW OFTEN we do something.
I often eat Chinese food.   I cook once a week.
These can be single words:
(100%) *always – usually – often – sometimes – never* (0%)
They <u>usually</u> go in the middle of the sentence:
I usually eat bread for breakfast. (between the subject and verb)
I'm always hungry. (after *be*)

They can also be phrases:
once a day (= one time) / *twice a day* (= two times) /
three times a day / *every day* / *every month* / *every year*

Phrases go at the end, or sometimes at the beginning of a sentence.
*I go to school **every day**. **Every day**, I go to school.*

A How are the people doing these things? Make adverbs with the words in the box.

careful	worried	messy	happy
hard	healthy		

1 She's making a cake _____.
2 They're talking and cooking _____.
3 He's cutting meat _____.
4 He's looking at the cook book _____.
5 She's cooking _____.
6 He's working _____.

KET **B** Choose the best word for each sentence.

1 I asked her _____ for the bread.
   A slowly   B dangerously   C politely
2 She makes interesting food. She cooks really _____ .
   A badly   B creatively   C nervously
3 The food was fantastic and I ate it _____ .
   A perfectly   B fast   C confidently
4 We waited _____ for the waiter.
   A patiently   B well   C wildly
5 She showed us her cake _____.
   A scarily   B safely   C proudly

C Put the words and phrases in brackets in the correct place. Draw arrows (→).

Example: (*every week*) Think of all the food you eat.

(1 *sometimes*) A lot of teenagers drink cola or similar drinks. (2 *usually*) And they eat some chocolate or candy. (3 *once or twice a week*) Most people eat eggs. (4 *every day*) And a lot of people drink milk.

(5 *every week*) Perhaps you know how much you eat and drink. (6 *never*) But most people think how much they eat and drink in a lifetime.

2 VOCABULARY

A **Write the food words for the definitions.**

1 You can make French fries from this vegetable.
p_____

2 It's white and many people eat it for breakfast.
y_____

3 You cook food with this or put it on salad.
o_____

4 They're long and thin and popular in Asian cooking.
n_____

5 Sometimes you cry when you cut this vegetable.
o_____

6 The juice of this yellow fruit is good with fish or in tea.
l_____

7 You put things in this to make sandwiches.
b_____

8 When you cut this fruit, it looks like a red heart.
s_____

9 You make this white or yellow food from milk.
c_____

10 This long green vegetable is good in salads.
c_____

B **Write the correct words.**

1 _____	6 _____
2 _____	7 _____
3 _____	8 _____
4 _____	9 _____
5 _____	10 _____

SMART TIP

Draw a picture with words from a word family. Learn the words with the picture. Close your eyes, so you can 'see' the picture and words together in your head.

C **Complete the sentences with the correct collocations. Use one word from each box.**

cook   burn   grow   read   order   weigh

food in a restaurant   50 kilos   meals calories   vegetables   food labels

1 We _____ in our garden.
2 You can _____ when you do sport.
3 I'm 160 cm and I _____.
4 I always _____ when I shop for food.
5 I can never decide when I _____.
6 I help to _____ at home.

D **Write the correct word or phrase from the box.**

always   three times a day   every day   twice a day   never   once a week

Marie ...

1 does sport (1 x week) _____ .
2 (0%) _____ eats meat.
3 eats fruit (Mon-Sun) _____ .
4 (100%) _____ drinks water with meals.
5 eats (3 x day) _____ .
6 cleans her teeth (2 x day) _____ .

MY WORDS FROM UNIT 10

1 _____
2 _____
3 _____
4 _____
5 _____

After Unit 11:
☐ I know these words. ☺
☐ I don't know these words. ☹ (Learn them again!)

3 COMMUNICATION

47 **A** **Put the conversation (a-h) in the correct order. Then listen and check.**

a What's your favourite food? ☐

b Vegetables? Well, I like peppers and olives. I hate carrots! ☐

c I love anything with pasta, especially pasta and tomato sauce. ☐

d OK. My favourite fruit's pineapple. I like pineapple juice too. ☐

e Pineapple juice? I don't like fruit juice. It's too sweet. ☐

f Mmm, I like pasta too. What about vegetables? ☐

g I don't know. I don't really have a favourite fruit. ☐

h Really? I love carrots! What's your favourite fruit? ☐

48 **B** **KET** **Complete the conversation. Write the correct letters (A–G) for 1–5. There are two extra sentences. Then listen and check.**

Girl So you play football. Are you good?

Boy (1) *C*

Girl I can't play football. I can't run very fast.

Boy (2) _____

Girl Yes, but the court is much smaller! How often do you play football?

Boy (3) _____

Girl That's hard. We only play matches once or twice a month.

Boy (4) _____

Girl I usually see my friends. Or I sometimes go shopping with my mum.

Boy (5) _____

Girl Sure, thanks.

A We train twice a week and then we have a match on Saturdays.

B I never play football.

C Not bad. I train really hard.

D What do you on Sundays?

E How often do you play basketball?

F But you play basketball really well. I saw you last week.

G Perhaps we can go out one Sunday?

4 PRONUNCIATION

49 **A** **Listen to the sentences. Pay attention to the pronunciation of the consonants at the end of the adverbs.**

I waited patie**ntly** in the line for school lunch.

I don't think I read the cook book corre**ctly**.

50 **B** **Listen to this story and pay attention to the adverbs. Then listen again and repeat the adverbs.**

I went to a local cheeseburger eating competition. I chose my first cheeseburger confide**ntly** and ca**lmly**. I ate three more burgers qui**ckly**. Then I ate another burger nervou**sly** and me**ssily**. I felt ill ... I didn't win and left the competition sa**dly**.

51 **C** **Listen to the sentence below again. Read it out loud five times as quickly as you can.**

I chose my first cheeseburger confidently and calmly.

SMART TIP

Say all the consonants in bold together. <u>Don't</u> put vowels between the consonants or after them.

5 CLIL

A Complete the facts with words in the box.

| thirsty | brain | sweat | headaches | kidneys |
| heart | blood | bones | | |

1 Boys _____ more than girls.
2 Your _____ beats about 100,000 times a day.
3 In one day, your _____ travels 19,000 km around your body.
4 Your _____ stop growing when you are about 25. (An adult has 206.)
5 The _____ has two halves: the right side is your creative side. The left side is your thinking side (good for maths and language).
6 Your body has two _____ – each one is the size of a computer mouse.
7 When you feel _____, your body already has too little water.
8 You can get _____ from eating ice-cream because it is so cold.

B Read about Kwan's health. Then write about your health.

My health, by Kwan

I think I'm quite healthy. I eat lots of different foods. I always eat lots of fruit and vegetables and fish. I never drink cola and I drink lots of water.

I do martial arts twice a week and I cycle to school.

I'm not ill very often but I sometimes get headaches. (My mum says that's because of computer games.)

My health, by _____

_____

_____

_____

_____

_____

_____

_____

6 PORTFOLIO WRITING

A Read Bianca's email. True (T) or false (F)?

1 Bianca eats everything. ☐
2 She eats cheese for breakfast. ☐
3 She eats a big meal at lunch. ☐
4 She comes from Spain. ☐
5 She doesn't eat a big meal in the evening. ☐
6 She wants to try American food. ☐

QUICK LINKS   SEARCH MAIL

Dear Mr and Mrs Harris

Thank you for your email. You asked me about food. I eat most things but I'm afraid I don't like mushrooms or potatoes.

Every day, I eat bread or toast for breakfast and sometimes cake. Lunch is the most important meal of the day in Italy. I usually eat pasta or meat with vegetables. In the evening, we eat eggs or soup or salad.

I'm looking forward to meeting you next week – and to eating American food. School in Seattle sounds great!

Best wishes

Bianca

B Find polite phrases in the email with these meanings:

1 I was happy you wrote.

_____

2 I'm sorry but ...

_____

3 I'm excited to see you.

_____

C **You also plan to stay with Mr and Mrs Harris in**
KET **Seattle. Write them an email (80-100 words). Use the polite phrases in B. Write:**

– what foods you don't eat (and why)
– what you usually eat for breakfast, lunch and dinner in your country
– what you want to do in Seattle

1 GRAMMAR

52 **A** **Complete Sam's loves and hates. Use the gerund (-ing) form of the words in the box.**

read	get up	take	watch	wait	listen
play	swim				

I like (1) _____ photos.
I love (2) _____ to music.
I like (3) _____ chess with my dad.
I love (4) _____ in the sea.
I hate (5) _____ early.
I don't like (6) _____ for things.
I don't like (7) _____ TV.
I prefer (8) _____ books.

B **Complete the dialogues with and or but.**

Aunt	Do you eat meat?
Lily	No, I never eat meat, (1) _____ I eat fish.
Aunt	What about cheese (2) _____ eggs?
Lily	Yes, I do, (3) _____ I don't like cheese much.
Friend's mum	Do you eat meat?
Tariq	Well, I eat beef (4) _____ I don't eat pork because of my religion.
Friend's mum	OK. We don't eat much meat (5) _____ we like chicken.
Tariq	I love chicken (6) _____ rice, we eat that a lot at home.

C **Put the words in the sentences in the correct order.**

1 sport / it's / every day / to do / important
2 basketball / three times a week / play / I
3 train / I / basketball / hard / and / I / really like
4 usually / to school / I / by bike / go
5 cycle / I have / really quickly / a racing bike / and / I
6 can / quite well / I / swim
7 go swimming / I / at the weekend / often
8 eat / I / healthily / try / and / too

2 VOCABULARY

A **Circle the odd word out for each VERB.**

Example:
WATCH the Olympics postcards TV football matches

1 MAKE clothes videos clouds cakes
2 COLLECT stamps coins chips key rings
3 PLAY baseball cycling cards hockey
4 DO athletics volleyball martial arts gymnastics
5 GO drawing riding ice-skating skiing

B **Complete the sports equipment for each sport.**

1 For table tennis, you need two b_____ and a table with a n_____ .
2 For (field) hockey, you need a hockey s_____ .
3 For cycling and skateboarding, you need to wear a h_____ .
4 For surfing, you need a b_____ .
5 For tennis, you need a tennis r_____ and some tennis b_____ .
6 For football, you need a football p_____ with two g_____ .

C **Put the foods in the box in the correct list.**

milk	fish	bacon	eggs	
carrots	beef	pineapple	cucumber	orange
juice	onions	rice	beans	pork
bananas	noodles	peppers	strawberries	
water	sausage	apples	pasta	tea
lemons	cola			

Fruit	Vegetables	Meat	Drinks
_____	_____	_____	_____
_____	_____	_____	_____
_____	_____	_____	_____
_____	_____	_____	_____
_____	_____		

Other

_____ _____ _____ _____

3 LISTENING KET

Listen to some information about a swimming pool. Complete questions 1–5.

Kingston Fun Pool

The pool costs £4 for two hours,

£6 for four hours

(1) and _____ for the whole day

You use the key to go in

(2) and for the _____

The cafeteria sells sandwiches, fruit

(3) and _____

The changing rooms for girls

(4) are on the _____

Before you swim

(5) you need to _____

4 READING KET

Read the text about breakfast. Are sentences 1–6 *Right* (A) or *Wrong* (B)?
If the text doesn't say this information, circle (C) *Doesn't say*.

The most important meal of the day

After a good night's sleep, it's important to give our bodies and our brains energy for the day ahead. A good breakfast stops you being tired. It also helps you to think better and do better in school. But surveys in both the USA and Scotland show that many teenagers don't eat breakfast at all.

In Scotland, most 11-year-old boys and girls usually eat breakfast. But only 58% of 15-year-old boys and 44.8% of 15-year-old girls always eat breakfast. And in the USA, only 36% of high school students eat breakfast every day. Many students say they don't eat breakfast because they don't have time or they don't feel hungry.

A healthy breakfast contains 25%–30% of the day's calories. You can burn off these calories during the day. When you don't eat breakfast, you usually eat more unhealthy snacks and fast food. So eating breakfast helps you not to become overweight.

1 Our brains and bodies need energy in the morning.
A Right   B Wrong   C Doesn't say

2 When you eat breakfast, you do better in school.
A Right   B Wrong   C Doesn't say

3 Most teenagers eat breakfast every day.
A Right   B Wrong   C Doesn't say

4 Many students don't have time for breakfast because they're doing their homework.
A Right   B Wrong   C Doesn't say

5 A healthy breakfast contains fruit.
A Right   B Wrong   C Doesn't say

6 If you eat breakfast, you usually become overweight.
A Right   B Wrong   C Doesn't say

1 GRAMMAR

going to future

To talk about future plans we use the *going to* future.
I'm **going to** *take exams next year.*   *He's* **going to** *be a doctor.*

We make the *going to* future with **be + (not) going to + verb**

Positive		Negative	
I'm (I am) he's (he is) / she's (she is) / it's (it is) we're (we are) / you're (you are) / they're (they are)	going to sleep	I'm not (am not) he / she / it **isn't (is not)** we / you / they **aren't (are not)**	going to sleep
Questions		**Short answers**	
Am I **Is** he / she / it **Are** you / we / they	going to sleep?	Yes, I am. / No, I'm not. Yes, she is. / No, she isn't. Yes, they are. / No, they aren't.	

We often use these time phrases with the *going to* future:
   tomorrow / the day after tomorrow/ at the weekend
   next Monday / week / month / year / summer   in two years / in 2020

A **Complete the sentences with the correct form of** *going to.*

1 Our class (make) _____ a glass window.
2 Each student (design) _____ a piece of glass in different colours.
3 Then we (make) _____ our designs.
4 I (do) _____ something in red and yellow.
5 My friends (use) _____ yellow and blue.
6 Then we (put) _____ our glass together to make the window.

SMART TIP

Remember that in conversation we use short forms (*I'm going to / she's going to* etc).

B **Joey's Dad isn't listening to him. Write Joey's sentences. Use the negative form of** *going to.*

1 **Dad:** So you're going to do a metal project.
   Joey: We _____ . It's a wood project.
2 **Dad:** And you're going to make a table.
   Joey: I _____ – I want to make a chair!
3 **Dad:** OK. So all the students are going to make chairs.
   Joey: No, all the students _____ . You can choose.

4 **Dad:** But your teacher's going to help.
   Joey: No, he _____. It's part of the exam.
5 **Dad:** Oh yes, right. It's going to be 10% of your exam.
   Joey: No, Dad, it _____ . It's going to be 20%!

C **Complete the dialogue with Shireen.**

Interviewer What (1 *you / make*) _____ today?

Shireen I (2 *make*) _____ a scrapbook page. I make pages about lots of different topics: my family, trips, ice cream ...

Interviewer And what (3 *this page / be*) _____ about?

Shireen Paris. We went on a trip to Paris last summer, so this page (4 *describe*) _____ that trip. My mum (5 *help*) _____ me.

Interviewer So what exactly (6 *you / do*) _____?

Shireen We (7 *cut out*) _____ some photos. And I (8 *use*) _____ parts of postcards too.

2 VOCABULARY

A Write the correct words.

Before I started school, I went to (1) n_____.
Then when I was five, I started (2) p_____ school.
I changed schools when I was eleven and started
(3) s_____ school. We did an important (4)
t_____ then. When I was in Year 11, I took my
GCSE (5) e_____. After GCSEs, you can leave
school, but I decided to study in the (6) s_____
f_____.

B Complete the sentences with the correct word from the box.

be	stay	think	do	go	travel
apply	retake				

Finn I think I want to (1) _____ round the world and see other countries.

Brit I'm good with my hands, so I'd like to (2) _____ an apprenticeship.

Tom I want to (3) _____ on at school and do A-levels. If I do badly in my GCSEs, I'd like to (4) _____ my exams.

Aziz I plan to (5) _____ for a job in an office.

Estela I'd like to (6) _____ to college and study art.

Matt I really want to (7) _____ a volunteer for a year – something to do with the environment.

Ayumi I don't know what I want to do. It's too early to (8) _____ about my future career.

SMART TIP

When you do an exercise like B in a test, check if the **verbs and nouns** go together. Remember to learn these **collocations** as phrases.

KET **C** Read and choose the best word for each space.

A survey in Britain showed students often feel
(1) _____ about exams. 63% say they need good
(2) _____ to get into college or university. 62%
(3) _____ about the questions in the exam. 59% say
their parents want good (4) _____. This makes it
hard for them to (5) _____ and do their best.

1	A excited	B bored	C stressed
2	A hair	B results	C friends
3	A learn	B worry	C read
4	A marks	B notes	C messages
5	A help	B travel	C relax

D Complete the poster with the correct words for the pictures.

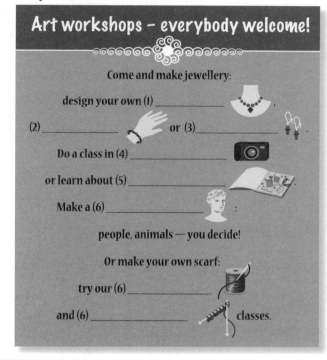

Art workshops – everybody welcome!

Come and make jewellery:

design your own (1) _____

(2) _____ or (3)_____

Do a class in (4) _____

or learn about (5) _____

Make a (6) _____ :

people, animals — you decide!

Or make your own scarf:

try our (6) _____

and (6) _____ classes.

MY WORDS FROM UNIT 11

1 _____

2 _____

3 _____

4 _____

5 _____

After Unit 12:
I know these words. ☐ ☺
I don't know these words. ☐ ☹ (Learn them again!)

3 COMMUNICATION

53 **A** **Luis is asking Vincenzo about school in Italy. Choose answer A, B or C. Then listen and check.**

1 When do you start school?
   A No, we don't.   B Usually at six.   C Every year.

2 When do you change schools?
   A When we're eleven.   B It's easy to change.
   C Yes, it's a big change.

3 When do you take exams?
   A Every day.   B When we're thirteen / fourteen and eighteen / nineteen.
   C Three times a week.

4 Do you do coursework?
   A No, just exams.   B I don't like work.
   C We have a lot of homework.

5 When can you leave school?
   A When you're six.   B When you're ten.
   C At fifteen or sixteen.

54 **B** **Read sentences (a–f). They are lines from two conversations. Write each conversation in the correct order. Then listen and check.**

a Yeah, OK. Thanks.
b Yes, but you can work and study at the same time.
c I think I'm going to go swimming. Do you want to come?
d I thought you need to go to college for that.
e Not much. What about you?
f I'm going to apply for a job in a zoo.

Conversation 1

A What are you going to do at the weekend?

B 1_____

A 2_____

B 3_____

Conversation 2

A What are you going to do when you leave school?

B 4_____

A 5_____

B 6_____

---

4 PRONUNCIATION

55 **A** **Listen to these sentences. Pay attention to the <u>stress</u> and the rhythm of the sentence. Then listen again and repeat.**

I'd <u>like</u> to <u>apply</u> for a <u>job</u>.

I <u>hope</u> to <u>study</u> at <u>college</u>.

56 **B** **Now listen to these sentences. <u>Underline</u> the stress.**

1 I plan to work in a school.

2 I'm interested in a lot of different things.

3 I want to travel round the world.

4 I'm going to work with children.

5 I'd like to do something different.

6 I'm going to think about my future.

56 **C** **Listen again to the sentences in B and repeat.**

SMART TIP

In English sentences, we stress the words with the most meaning. Usually these are nouns, verbs and adjectives.

5 CLIL

A Complete the question and answers with the correct words from the box.

> author   source   essay
> cut and paste   quote   copy

QUICK LINKS [ ]   SEARCH MAIL [ ]

Question

I was really worried about my homework. So I decided to
(1) _____ an
(2) _____ off the internet.
Is that OK?

Answers

Sara: You can (3) _____
some sentences but you must give the
(4) _____'s name and the
name of the article. 👍

Scott: No! It is never OK to do
that when you don't give the
(5) _____ of information. 👍

Claire: Next time (6) _____
bits from different websites (so your
teacher can't check). 👎

B Write your tips for writing essays.

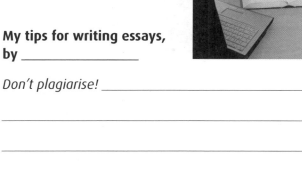

**My tips for writing essays,
by _____**

Don't plagiarise! _____

_____

_____

_____

_____

_____

6 PORTFOLIO WRITING

A Read Dylan's status on his social media page. Answer the questions.

1   What's he going to do on Saturday?
2   What's he going to do on Sunday? Is he looking forward to this?

> On Saturday, I plan to sleep in as usual and then just hang out at home. My brother and I are going to watch a film in the evening. Jack and Robbie are going to come round on Sunday and we're going to go karting with Dad. Check out the photo of us last time. It was amazing. I can't wait to try it again! Really excited!

B Find phrases in Dylan's status with these meanings:

1   stay in bed for a long time in the morning

_____

2   in the same way as most of the time

_____

3   I'm really looking forward to this.

_____

C Write your 'status' for today. Write about your
KET plans for the weekend (50–80 words). Write about:

– what you're going to do on Saturday
– what you're going to do on Sunday
– how you feel about these plans

1 GRAMMAR

Present perfect

Use the **present perfect + ever / never** to talk about experiences in your life – from the *past* to the *present*.

I've never **watched** a baseball match.   **Have** you ever **volunteered**?

We make the present perfect with **have + past participle** (watched, volunteered).
We make the past participle of regular verbs with **–ed**.
Learn the past participle of irregular verbs. (See page 144 in the Student's Book.)

Positive	Negative
I've (I **have**) he's / she's /it's (he **has**) tried we're / you're / they've (we **have**)	I **haven't** (**have not**) he / she / it **hasn't** (**has not**) tried we / you / they **haven't** (**have not**)
Questions	Short answers
Have I **Has** he / she / it **tried**? **Have** you / we / they	Yes, I have. / No, I haven't. Yes, she has. / No, she hasn't. Yes, they have. / No, they haven't.

have been

We use *been* (past participle of *be*) to talk about travel experiences or sports activities:

I've **been** to the USA.   *I've* **been skiing** three times.

Don't use *gone* (past participle of *go*). He's gone to the USA. (= He went there and he's still there.)

A **Complete the text with the correct past participle.**

Story Musgrave has (1 *do*) _____ lots
of different things in his life. He's (2 *fly*)
_____ planes and (3 *make*) _____
over 800 parachute jumps. He's (4 *be*) _____
an astronaut and he's (5 *walk*) _____ in space.
He's (6 *travel*) _____ to space six times! He's
also (7 *study*) _____ seven different subjects
at university. He's (8 *work*) _____ as a doctor, he's
(9 *grow*) _____ palm trees and he's (10 *teach*)
_____ students.

B **Write the questions for a questionnaire. Use**
Have you ever ...?

1 call / a teacher 'Mum' or 'Dad' by mistake
Have you ever _____ ?

2 break / your arm
_____ ?

3 drive / a car
_____ ?

4 watch / a play
_____ ?

5 eat / Mexican food
_____ ?

6 lose / some money
_____ ?

7 sleep / in a tent
_____ ?

8 laugh and cry / at the same time
_____ ?

C **Look at Felipe's answers to the questionnaire**
in B. Write the things he has done (✓) and he
hasn't done (✗).

1 ✗ He hasn't _____

2 ✓ _____

3 ✗ _____

4 ✗ _____

5 ✓ _____

6 ✓ _____

7 ✗ _____

8 ✓ _____

2 VOCABULARY

A Complete the dialogues with the correct words.

| animal shelter | garage sale | charity shop |
| festival | homeless shelter | |

A What are we going to do for Charity Week at school?

B We could volunteer at the (1) _____ . They always need people to prepare food.

A What about the (2) _____? We could take the dogs for walks.

B Yes, or we could also volunteer in the (3) _____ in town. It sells all sorts of stuff.

A Or we could have a (4) _____ and give the money to charity.

B Good idea! We could sell our old stuff at the school (5) _____ next week too.

KET **B** Which notice (1-6) says this (A-F)?

1 No picnics or barbecues on the grass!

2 Bowling every day from 12:00 - 22:00

3 Green Farm: No hiking through the fields!

4 Art exhibition now until Friday 28th

5 No water fights please.

6 Entrance to sports events with tickets only.

A You can't play in the pool. ☐
B You can't see matches without paying. ☐
C You can't eat here. ☐
D You can't walk here. ☐
E You can do this sport in the afternoons. ☐
F You can see pictures and sculptures here. ☐

C Read and choose the best word for each space.

KET

I've done all three (1) _____ of the Duke of Edinburgh programme. First I did bronze. I really enjoyed it so I did (2) _____ next. Then after that, I did the hardest level, (3)_____ . I got that (4) _____ at Buckingham Palace in London. I especially remember the three-day (5)_____ and I still go hiking sometimes.

1	A areas	B courses	C levels
2	A silver	B nothing	C event
3	A last	B skill	C gold
4	A prize	B competition	C award
5	A volunteers	B expeditions	C festivals

D Complete the words in the facts with *a, e, i, o* or *u*.

1 Yuri Gagarin was the first person to travel into sp__c__.

2 Valentina Tereshkova was the first woman __str__n__ __t in space.

3 Neil Armstrong was the first person to walk on the m__ __n.

4 The last flight of the American space sh__ttl__ programme was in 2011.

5 Half of space travellers feel sick when they become w__ __ghtl__ss.

6 The pl__n__t Mars gets its name from the Roman god of war.

MY WORDS FROM UNIT 12

1 _____
2 _____
3 _____
4 _____
5 _____

Check them:
☐ I know these words. ☺
☐ I don't know these words. ☹ (Learn them again!)

3 COMMUNICATION

57 **A** **Put the conversations in the right order. Write 1, 2, 3, 4 in the boxes. Then listen and check.**

1 a Well, it looks easier on TV! ☐
   b I went snowboarding for the first time. ☐
   c What did you do in the last winter holidays? ☐
   d Was it hard? ☐

2 a I just hung out with friends and relaxed. ☐
   b Yeah, but we went shopping at the mall too. ☐
   c At home? ☐
   d What did you do last weekend? ☐

3 a Did you go on holiday? ☐
   b What did you do last summer? ☐
   c No, but we went on lots of day trips. ☐
   d Lots of things. We had barbecues, picnics, went swimming ... ☐

58 **B** **Match the questions and answers. Choose A, B, or C.**

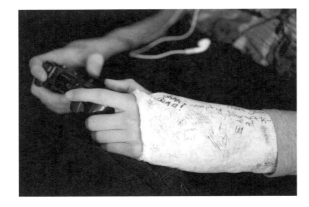

1 Have you ever broken your arm?
   A Yes, it really hurt.   B No, I never drop things.
   C Yes, tomorrow.
2 Have you ever eaten noodles?
   A No, I don't like fruit.   B No, I haven't.
   C No, I'm really hungry.
3 Have you ever been skiing?
   A Yes, I'm going to try it next week.
   B Yes, the water was really warm.
   C No, I've never been skiing.
4 Have you even won an award?
   A No, I didn't win. B Yes, two years ago, at school.
   C No, thanks.
5 Have you ever visited Japan?
   A Yes, I have.   B Yes, it looks great in photos.
   C No, I've never been to Europe.

4 PRONUNCIATION

59 **A** **Look at the sentences. The first sentence has 'normal' stress. In the other sentences, the stress is on a different word. The stress emphasises this word. Listen and repeat the sentences.**

1 My dad bought two tickets for the match against Brazil.
2 <u>My dad</u> bought two tickets for the match against Brazil. (*My dad bought them, not me.*)
3 My dad <u>bought</u> two tickets for the match against Brazil. (*My dad bought them; they weren't free.*)
4 My dad bought <u>two</u> tickets for the match against Brazil. (*not one ticket*)
5 My dad bought two tickets for the match against <u>Brazil</u>. (*not against Argentina*)

60 **B** **Listen to another sentence. First listen to the sentence with normal stress (sentence 1). Then listen and <u>underline</u> the stress in sentences 2–5.**

1 My friend <u>Maria</u> has swum with <u>dolphins</u> in the Pacific Ocean.
2 My friend Maria has swum with dolphins in the Pacific Ocean.
3 My friend Maria has swum with dolphins in the Pacific Ocean.
4 My friend Maria has swum with dolphins in the Pacific Ocean.
5 My friend Maria has swum with dolphins in the Pacific Ocean.

61 **C** **Now match the questions to the answers (2–5) in exercise B. Look at the stress. Then listen and check.**

a Who has swum with dolphins? ☐
b What has she swum with? ☐
c What has she done with dolphins? ☐
d What ocean has she swum in? ☐

5 CLIL

A Read and complete each space with one word.

(1) G_____ works in the same way everywhere: it (2) p_____ objects towards each other.

On (3) E_____, gravity keeps your feet on the ground. In space, gravity means that our planet moves around the (4) S_____ . And it means that the (5) M_____ moves around the Earth.

Astronauts (6) f_____ in space because there's little gravity there.

B Write about your favourite space story or film. Use the questions to help you.

What's your favourite film called?
Who is in it? (astronauts / space travellers / people from other planets)
Where are they? (in space / on the Moon / in a space shuttle)
What happens? (the astronauts meet ... / they find ... / there's a fight)

_____

_____

_____

_____

_____

_____

_____

6 PORTFOLIO WRITING

A Read the question on a blog and Ellie's comment. What does she recommend and what doesn't she recommend. Why?

> **It's nearly the summer holidays and I'm looking for some new activities to do. What summer activity can you recommend? What activity can't you recommend? Why?**
>
> **Ellie's comment:**
>
> Have you ever played mini golf? I can recommend it. You can go with a group of friends or your family and it's great fun. I've played it five or six times now. There are mini golf places in lots of parks and it isn't expensive to play. Just be careful with your golf club! I hit my best friend in the face!
>
> Don't go fishing! I went with my uncle last summer and we sat by the river for four hours. We caught a few fish, but it was pretty boring. The only good thing is it's free (but you need the equipment, of course).
>
> *Ellie*

B In Ellie's comment, find phrases with these meanings:

1 to recommend something

_____

2 to not recommend something

_____

3 to say something could be dangerous

_____

4 to give one positive comment only

_____

C Write a comment on the blog about two summer
KET activities (80–100 words). Say:

– if you can recommend or not recommend them
– why or why not
– something about your personal experiences with them

1 GRAMMAR

A Complete the dialogue with the correct form of *going to*.

Emma Hi Cristos. What (1 you / do) _____ this evening?

Cristos Nothing special. My dad and I (2 make) _____ dinner and then I think I (3 watch) _____ TV. (4 you / get) _____ the bus home now?

Emma No, not today. I (5 meet) _____ Nisha in the library. She (6 help) _____ me fill in forms for volunteer jobs. We (7 not go) _____ on holiday this year because dad (8 not have) _____ much free time. So I'm looking for a summer job.

B Complete Shing's description of a festival visit. Use the correct irregular past simple forms.

I (1 *go*) _____ to the Harbin Ice Festival in Heilongjiang in China with my family last year. The festival (2 *begin*) _____ in 1963 and it's quite famous. We (3 *fly*) _____ from Beijing and then (4 *take*) _____ a bus to Harbin. I (5 *feel*) _____ really cold when we (6 *get*) _____there – it was -30 degrees! We (7 *see*) _____ some amazing ice sculptures: buildings, animals and people. Thousands of people (8 *come*) _____ to the festival. They (9 *make*) _____ the sculptures with snow and ice from the river. At night, the sculptures had different colour lights inside them. There was also an ice Great Wall and we (10 *run*) _____ up and down it. That was great fun!

C Write the questions and answers. Use the present perfect.

1 you / ever / forgot / to do your homework?
– yes / I / forgot / to do my homework / lots of times
_____
_____

2 your parents / ever / do / your homework for you?
– no / they / never / do / that
_____
_____

3 a teacher / ever / shout / at you?
– yes / she / shout / at me / once
_____

4 you / ever / fail / an exam?
– no / I / never / fail / an exam
_____
_____

5 your best friend / ever / copy / your homework?
– no / he / never / copy / my homework
_____
_____

2 VOCABULARY

A Match the verbs and nouns. Then complete sentences 1–6 with the correct collocations.

a	pass	school
b	apply for	at school
c	do	college
d	travel	schools
e	change	an apprenticeship
f	stay on	around the world
g	leave	a job
h	go to	your exams

1 In my country, students _____ after they finish primary school.

2 Students can _____ when they are 16.

3 A lot of students _____ to prepare for a university education.

4 If you don't _____, you can retake them a year later.

5 Some students want a practical job and _____.

6 Today it's very popular to _____ and learn about life in different countries.

B Match the correct description (a–e) for each quote (1–5).

1 'Yes! I'm so happy!' ☐

2 'When I look at the paper, I get nervous and can't think.' ☐

3 'We have so much homework and I never have time to do everything.' ☐

4 'I hope I didn't fail.' ☐

5 'I'm lying on my bed and listening to music.' ☐

    a She feels worried in exams.

    b She's trying to relax.

    c She feels stressed.

    d She's waiting for her exam results.

    e She's got good marks in her exams.

C Complete the activities.

1 It was so hot, we had a w_____ f_____ in the garden and got very wet.
2 There was a big f_____ at the weekend – fantastic music.
3 We went b_____ at the sports centre yesterday. I won!
4 We had a g_____ s_____ last week and sold lots of old stuff.
5 My mum volunteers in a c_____ s_____ on Saturdays. They sell old clothes and books.
6 I love dogs, so I volunteer in an a_____ s_____.
7 Yesterday my parents went to the opening of an a_____ e_____ by a local artist.
8 My friend had a b_____ for his birthday on the beach. There was a lot of food!

62 Listen to five short conversations. There is one question for each conversation.
For questions 1-5, tick (✓) the correct right answer.

1 Where are the boy and girl going to meet?

 A  B  C

2 Which man is the girl's geography teacher?

 A   B 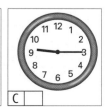 C

3 What time do students need to be in the main hall?

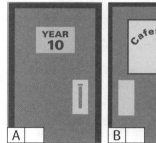 A  B  C

4 What does the boy offer to do with his friend?

 A  B  C

5 What did the girl get in her English test?

 A  B  C

Read the advert and the text message. Complete the form.

UNDERAGE FESTIVAL

The next underage music festival is on August 5th in Victoria Park, London E2.

Tickets: £31.50. On sale now! Order and collect from Stargreen Box office, Argyll Street, London W1F.

Remember: Age 13-17. No adults 18 or over.

ALFIE 7803583071

Tim, can you order me two tickets for the festival when you're at the box office this afternoon? (Don't forget I'm 16 now!) Thanks ☺

TICKET ORDER FORM

Name	Alfie Williams
Telephone number	_____
Age	_____
Event and date	_____
Number of tickets	_____
Total price	_____

Unit 1 Home life

 3 **COMMUNICATION**

 A

Girl 1: Do you have brothers and sisters?
Girl 2: Yes, two sisters.
Girl 1: How old are they?
Girl 2: Sixteen and eighteen.
Girl 1: Do you share a room with your sisters?
Girl 2: No, I don't. Do you have brothers or sisters?
Girl 1: I have a sister and a little half-brother.
Girl 2: A half-brother?
Girl 1: Yes, I live with my mum and my stepfather.
Girl 2: Do you like your stepfather?
Girl 1: Yes, he's great.
Girl 2: That's good.

 B

Conversation 1
Boy 1: What time do you get up?
Boy 2: Very early.
Boy 1: When do you have breakfast?
Boy 2: About seven o'clock.

Conversation 2
Girl: What time do you finish school?
Boy: At three o'clock in the afternoon.
Girl: What do you do in the evening?
Boy: I watch TV.

4 **PRONUNCIATION**

 A

sister, brother**s**, **sh**are

6 **B**

parent**s**, **s**ixteen, breakfa**st**, **s**tepfather, **s**leep
mu**s**ic, hi**s**, cou**s**in, friend**s**, ea**s**y
Engli**sh**, fini**sh**, **sh**ort, pronunciation, **sh**ower

Unit 2 Cool schools

3 **COMMUNICATION**

 A

Girl: I see you're at Churchill School.
Boy: How do you know that?
Girl: Your uniform! Do you like it there?
Boy: Well, not the uniform! But yes, it's OK.
Girl: I go to Westpark High.
Boy: Right, is that the new school near the park?
Girl: Yeah, that's right. I like it there.

Boy: It looks nice, very modern.
Girl: Yes, the classrooms and everything are all new.
Boy: Are the teachers nice?
Girl: Yes, they're OK.

 B

Conversation 1
Boy: Where are you from?
Girl: From Italy.
Boy: Where do you live?
Girl: Near the school.
Boy: How do you go to school?
Girl: I walk.
Boy: Do you like school?
Girl: No, I don't.
Boy: What's your favourite subject?
Girl: IT.

Conversation 2
Girl: Where are you from?
Boy: I'm English.
Girl: Where do you live?
Boy: About two kilometres from here.
Girl: How do you go to school?
Boy: By bus.
Girl: Do you like school?
Boy: It's OK.
Girl: What's your favourite subject?
Boy: Geography.

4 **PRONUNCIATION**

 A, B

1 What's your name?
2 Where's your school?
3 Who's your favourite teacher?
4 When's the English lesson?

11 **C, D**

1 Who's your best friend?
2 When's your birthday?
3 Where's your house?
4 What's your phone number?

Revision 1-2

12

1 **Teacher:**	Thomas … what time is it?
Thomas:	Er, twenty to nine, Ms Brown.
Headteacher:	And what time does school start?
Thomas:	Er, twenty past eight, miss.
Headteacher:	Exactly. Go to your class now. Come and see me in the break at 10 o'clock.

2 **Girl:** So where do you live?

Boy: Do you know the flats next to the cinema?
Girl: Yes, do you live there?
Boy: No, but near the flats there's a small white house. There's a caravan in the garden. I live in that house.
Girl: Oh, OK, the white house.

3 **Boy:** You don't eat a lot at lunch.
Girl: No, I have a big breakfast, so I usually just eat fruit for lunch. We always have a big dinner in the evening too.
Boy: Mmm. I have a big breakfast, a big lunch AND a big dinner.

4 **Girl:** But Dad, I don't want to move. What about school?
Dad: It's OK, you can stay at your school. The new flat is about four kilometres from here.
Girl: Four kilometres?
Dad: Yes, you can take the bus. It takes 14 or 15 minutes.

5 **Aunt:** … and what's your favourite subject at school? Maths?
Boy: No, it's geography.
Aunt: Biology? Oh, yes, you like animals …
Boy: No, not biology, geography, Aunt Bertha.

Unit 3 Hangouts

3 **COMMUNICATION**

 A

1 I often hang out at the shopping mall. There are a lot of things to do.
2 I usually hang out with school friends. But sometimes I hang out with my sister.
3 I sometimes go to the cinema. But only when there's a good film.
4 I often hang out with my friends online. We chat on Facebook.

14 **B**

Conversation 1
Girl: Excuse me, how do I get to the police station?
Adult: It's in Queen Street.
Girl: Where's Queen Street?
Adult: Go past the library and turn left. The police station is on the right.
Girl: Thank you.

Conversation 2
Boy: Excuse me, is there a bank near here?

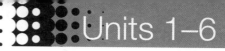

Adult: Yes, there's one in King's Road.
Boy: How do I get to King's Road?
Adult: Go straight on and turn right at the cinema. The bank is on the left.
Boy: Thank you.

 A

problem, boxing
go, show

 B, C

online, hospital, across, problem, opposite, office, offer, kilometre
clothes, hotel, postcard, home, know, role, photo, over

Unit 4 Not just a job

3 COMMUNICATION

A

 Conversation 1

Boy: What does your mum do?
Girl: She works at a hospital
Boy: What sort of work does she do?
Girl: Tests and things like that.

 Conversation 2

Girl: What does your dad do?
Boy: He's a writer. He writes for a magazine.
Girl: Cool. Does he work at home?
Boy: No, he has an office in town.

 Conversation 3

Boy: Does your brother have a job?
Girl: No, he doesn't.
Boy: What does he want to do?
Girl: He'd like to be an engineer.

 B

1 Can you cross your eyes?
   Yes, I can. It's funny.
2 Can you stand on your head?
   Yes, I can. But not for long.
3 Can you sing?
   No, I can't. I sound horrible.
4 Can you do martial arts?
   No I can't. I'm not good at sport.
5 Can you tell jokes?
   Yes, I can. Do you know the one about the farmer?
6 Can you eat five pizzas?
   No, I can't. And I don't want to do this.

4 PRONUNCIATION

 A Listen to the sounds.

She's a writer.
He's an explorer.

 B

1 He's a police officer.
2 She's an engineer.
3 He's a farmer.
4 She's a doctor.
5 He's a teacher.
6 She's a cleaner.
7 He's a driver.
8 She's an actor.

 C

She works at a hospital.
He works in an office.

 D

1 She works in a theatre.
2 I work in a factory.
3 They work at a police station.
4 He works at a school.
5 They work in a restaurant.
6 We work on a farm.

Revision 3-4

 Boy: What do your parents do again?

Girl: Well, my mum works in a clothes shop. She's a shop assistant. And my dad works at the hospital.
Boy: Oh, your dad's a doctor?
Girl: No, he isn't a doctor. He's a nurse, actually.
Boy: What about your brother?
Girl: Ben's a driver for a taxi company at the moment. He wants to be a police officer, but his health isn't very good.
Boy: Oh, OK. So your brother Ben's a taxi driver ... but your sister ... er, what's her name, Alice?
Girl: Yes, Alice.
Boy: She is a police officer, right?
Girl: No, no, that's my other sister, Gina. Gina loves her job. She's a great police officer.
Boy: So what does Alice do?
Girl: She's a fire fighter.
Boy: Wow, a police officer and a fire fighter. That's cool.

Unit 5 Scary stories

3 COMMUNICATION

 A

1 What's the weather like?
   It's rainy and cold.
2 What's the temperature today?
   It's about twenty degrees.
3 It is warm today?
   Yes, it's a really nice day.

4 What was the weather like in your area yesterday?
   It was sunny.
5 Do I need a jacket?
   Yes, it's a bit cold.

 B

It was in the autumn. It was the 31st of October.
It was very late. It was nearly midnight.
I wasn't in bed. I wasn't tired.
And I was bored. There was nothing on TV.
Outside it was stormy. And inside it was cold.
Suddenly, there was a loud noise. What was it?
Was it the front door? Was somebody in the house?
I was very quiet. And I was very scared.
And then there was another noise. It was very near now.
Was I alone? Or was somebody there...

4 PRONUNCIATION

 A

stormy
cloudy

 C, D

wall, information, bored, story, law, sport, daughter
tower, outside, down, sound, now, brown, flower

Unit 6 Tech time

3 COMMUNICATION

 A

Adult: What do you do in your free time, Jayden?
Boy: I go on the internet.
   I go on Facebook and I chat with my friends.
   I watch videos on YouTube.
   I play computer games.
Adult: What do you do in your free time, Logan?
Boy: I play the guitar.
   I write ideas and stories in my journal.
   I write my own songs.
   Sometimes I paint or draw.

 B

Claudia: In this photo, you can see me and my friends. We're in Baqueira Veret ski resort. We're standing on one of the mountains and we're resting for a bit. It's cold but it's sunny.

Blanca This is a photo of my best friends and me. We're at the stadium of Español FC. We're sitting where the manager and the players usually sit. It's winter, so it isn't very warm.

4 PRONUNCIATION

 A

watch, gadget

 B, C

1 She's checking her charger.
2 They're chatting about technology.
3 He's changing his jeans.
4 We're watching a band on stage.
5 He's writing a message in his journal.
6 She's choosing a new jacket.

 D

check chat change journal jacket jeans

Revision 5-6

36 **Ruby:** Hey, Luca, you're a boy …

Luca: Erm, yes …

Ruby: Well, my cousin is visiting. He's here for two weeks because my aunt and uncle are on holiday.

Luca: And?

Ruby: I don't know what to do with him. I don't know him that well … I don't see him very often.

Luca: Do some sport … like, you know, you can play basketball and football in the park.

Ruby: But I can't play basketball OR football.

Luca: Well, try swimming. Everyone likes swimming.

Ruby: I don't. I hate swimming.

Luca: Oh … erm … I know, what about video games?

Ruby: We don't have a games console, and I don't have a computer.

Luca: You don't have a games console? Wow. … Erm … Oh, I know. At the weekend, there's a film festival, you can watch films all day from 8 in the morning to 2 at night.

Ruby: Oh, yes, the film festival – of course! How much are the tickets do you know?

Luca: Quite cheap, about £3 a film, I think. Check the website on the internet – there's a programme too.

Ruby: Yes, great. Thanks, Luca.

Unit 7 Spend or Save?

3 COMMUNICATION

37 **A**

1 Girl: Excuse me.
Sales assistant: Yes, can I help you?
Girl: How much are these jeans?
Sales assistant: I think they're £50. Let me check.
2 Girl: Can I try these on?
Sales assistant: Yes, of course.
Girl: Erm, where's the changing room?
Sales assistant: Oh, sorry, it's over there.
3 Girl: Do you have this jacket in black?
Sales assistant: No, sorry, only in brown.
Girl: OK. Do you have it in small?
Sales assistant: Small? Yes, … here you are.

38 **B**

1 **A:** Do you like those trainers?
  B: Yes, but they're the most expensive in the shop!

2 **A:** Is your mum older than your dad?
  B: Yes, he's 40 and she's 45.

3 **A:** Is this the smallest size you have?
  B: No, I think we have a smaller size.

4 **A:** Are you the tallest in your family?
  B: No, I'm the shortest.

5 **A:** Are they your favourite boots?
  B: Yes, they're the most uncomfortable boots ever, but they look great!

4 PRONUNCIATION

 A

Her stylist has all the best and trendiest stuff.

B

style stuff story statement
student star stand start stop
stage

C

cost interest best trendiest
artist last easiest smallest worst
fastest

D

strong street strict strange
straight stretch

Unit 8 Holidays!

3 COMMUNICATION

40 **A**

In my last holidays I went on holiday to Italy. I went with my parents and my sister.

We were in a little town by the sea. We had a holiday apartment there.

We were in the water a lot. We went swimming and water skiing.

We usually ate in the apartment but sometimes we went to restaurants. The food was really good.

At home Italian food is always pizza and pasta. But on holiday we tried lots of other things.

B

A: Something really embarrassing happened to me yesterday.
B: OK … Where were you?
A: At my cousin's party.
B: So what happened?
A: I fell over somebody's leg and then I fell on this really pretty girl.
B: Mmm, a bit embarrassing. What did you do then?
A: Well, I went bright red. And then I asked her out.
B: You what? You asked her out?
A: Yeah. And she said yes.
B: Wow, I need to try that!

4 PRONUNCIATION

41

Italy **Sw**eden
tour**i**st **e**cotourism

B

brilliant **sea** prison English
f**ie**ld tr**i**p theme park ten**ni**s
b**ea**ch **ea**t dolphin hill sn**ee**ze
Pacific sight**see**ing sl**ee**p

C

Column 1: brilliant, prison, English, trip, tennis, dolphin, hill, Pacific

Column 2: sea, field, theme park, beach, eat, sneeze, sightseeing, sleep

WB Revision 7-8

Shop assistant: Hello, can I help you?

Girl: Yes, do you have the jacket in the window in black?

Shop assistant: Yes, we do. We have it in brown, grey and black.

Girl: Oh, great. How much is it?

Shop assistant: It's usually £44.50 but there's ten pounds off this week so it's £34.50.

Girl: That's lucky! I really like it.

Shop assistant: What size do you need?

Girl: Small.

Shop assistant: Oh ... just let me check ... No, I'm afraid we don't have that size in black – or in brown. We have a small in grey.

Girl: No, I really wanted it in black.

Shop assistant: I can order it for you.

Girl: Can you? Yes, please.

Shop assistant: What's your name and phone number?

Girl: Julia Flowers, 2348792.

Shop assistant: 2348792?

Girl: Yes, that's right.

Shop assistant: OK, it usually takes 2 or 3 days.

Girl: That's fine. Thanks for your help.

Unit 9 Loves and hates

3 COMMUNICATION

 A

1 **A:** What's your favourite sport?
B: I love swimming.
2 **A:** Are you in a team or club?
B: I'm a member of the tennis club.
3 **A:** Do you support a team or a club?
B: No, I don't.
4 **A:** Do you watch sport?
B: I sometimes go to volleyball matches.
5 **A:** Why do you like this sport?
B: I'm good at it.

 B

1 **A:** Do you like watching TV?

B: Yes, I do, especially films. What about you?
A: I prefer listening to music.
B: I like listening to music too.
2 **A:** I hate tidying my room.
B: Me too! I hate doing stuff in the house.
A: Mmm, sometimes I quite like cooking.
B: Oh, no, I hate cooking.
3 **A:** What sports do you like?
B: I love skiing.
A: Really? I can't ski.
B: It's easy, you should try it!

4 PRONUNCIATION

 A

A: Do you play football and hockey?
B: I don't play <u>football,</u> but I play <u>hockey</u>.
A: Do you like skiing and water skiing?
B: I like <u>skiing,</u> but I don't like <u>water skiing</u>.

 B

1 You don't play tennis with a bat; you play it with a racket.
2 I don't collect stamps; I collect coins.
3 He isn't in the basketball team; he's in the baseball team.
4 She isn't a snowboarder; she's a skateboarder.
5 I don't make model planes; I make model boats.
6 We don't play football; we watch it.

Unit 10 Live to eat?

3 COMMUNICATION

 A

A: What's your favourite food?
B: I love anything with pasta, especially pasta and tomato sauce.
A: Mmm, I like pasta too. What about vegetables?
B: Vegetables? Well, I like peppers and olives. I hate carrots!
A: Really? I love carrots! What's your favourite fruit?
B: I don't know. I don't really have a favourite fruit.
A: OK. My favourite fruit's pineapple. I like pineapple juice too.
B: Pineapple juice? I don't like fruit juice. It's too sweet.

 B

Girl: So you play football. Are you good?
Boy: Not bad. I train really hard.
Girl: I can't play football. I can't run very fast.

Boy: But you play basketball really well. I saw you last week.
Girl: Yes, but the court is much smaller! How often do you play football?
Boy: We train twice a week and then we have a match on Saturdays.
Girl: That's hard. We only play matches once or twice a month.
Boy: What do you on Sundays?
Girl: I usually see my friends. Or I sometimes go shopping with my mum.
Boy: Perhaps we can go out one Sunday?
Girl: Sure, thanks.

4 PRONUNCIATION

I waited patie**ntly** in the line for school lunch.
I don't think I read the cook book corre**ctly**.

I went to a local cheeseburger eating competition. I chose my first cheeseburger confide**ntly** and ca**lmly**. I ate three more burgers qui**ckly**. Then I ate another burger nervou**sly** and mess**ily**. I felt ill. I didn't win and left the competition sa**dly**.

51

I chose my first cheeseburger confidently and calmly.

WB Revision 9-10

52

Let me give you some information about the swimming pool. The pool costs £4 for two hours, £6 for four hours or £10 for the whole day. This is your key – you pay when you come out. You use your key to go in and you can use it for the cafeteria. The cafeteria is at the back of the pool area. You can buy snacks like sandwiches, fruit and yoghurt there. The cafeteria doesn't sell burgers or chips, I'm afraid. You pay for food and drinks when you come out.

Now, to go to the swimming pool, go straight on here. The changing rooms for boys are on the left and for girls on the right. You use your key for the lockers for your clothes and other things. Before you swim, remember to have a shower. And please look after your key and don't lose it in the pool! OK? Enjoy your swim!

Unit 11 Learning for life

3 COMMUNICATION

A

1 A: When do you start school?
B: Usually at six.
2 A: When do you change schools?
B: When we're eleven.
3 A: When do you take exams?
B: When we're thirteen / fourteen and eighteen / nineteen.
4 A: Do you do coursework?
B: No, just exams.
5 A: When can you leave school?
B: At fifteen or sixteen.

B

Conversation 1
A: What are you going to do at the weekend?
B: Not much. What about you?
A: I think I'm going to go swimming. Do you want to come?
B: Yeah, OK. Thanks.

Conversation 2
A: What are you going to do when you leave school?
B: I'm going to apply for a job in a zoo.
A: I thought you need to go to college for that.
B: Yes, but you can work and study at the same time.

4 PRONUNCIATION

A

I'd <u>like</u> to <u>apply</u> for a <u>job</u>.
I <u>hope</u> to <u>study</u> at <u>college</u>.

B / C

1 I plan to work in a school.
2 I'm interested in a lot of different things.
3 I want to travel round the world.
4 I'm going to work with children.
5 I'd like to do something different.
6 I'm going to think about my future.

Unit 12 Events and experiences

3 COMMUNICATION

 A

1 A: What did you do in the last winter holidays?
B: I went snowboarding for the first time.

A: Was it hard?
B: Well, it looks easier on TV!
2 A: What did you do last weekend?
B: I just hung out with friends and relaxed.
A: At home?
B: Yeah, but we went shopping at the mall too.
3 A: What did you do last summer?
B: Lots of things. We had barbecues, picnics, went swimming ...
A: Did you go on holiday?
B: No, but we went on lots of day trips.

B

1 Have you ever broken your arm?
Yes, it really hurt.
2 Have you ever eaten noodles?
No, I haven't.
3 Have you ever been skiing?
No, I've never been skiing.
4 Have you ever won an award?
Yes, two years ago at school.
5 Have you ever visited Japan?
Yes, I have.

4 PRONUNCIATION

A

1 My dad bought two tickets for the match against Brazil.
2 *My dad* bought two tickets for the match against Brazil.
3 My dad *bought* two tickets for the match against Brazil.
4 My dad bought *two* tickets for the match against Brazil.
5 My dad bought two tickets for the match against *Brazil*.

B

1 My friend Maria has swum with dolphins in the Pacific Ocean.
2 My friend Maria has swum with dolphins in the Pacific Ocean.
3 My friend Maria has swum with dolphins in the Pacific Ocean.
4 My friend Maria has swum with dolphins in the Pacific Ocean.
5 My friend Maria has swum with dolphins in the Pacific Ocean.

C

a Who has swum with dolphins?
My friend <u>Maria</u>.
b What has she swum with?
She's swum with <u>dolphins</u>.
c What has she done with dolphins?
She's <u>swum</u> with dolphins.
d What ocean has she swum in?
She's swum in the <u>Pacific</u> Ocean.

WB Revision 11-12

1 Boy: When are you going to do the maths homework?
Girl: Erm, I don't know. Why?
Boy: I don't understand it. ... Can we do it together?
Girl: Sure ... erm, what about the free lesson after lunch? In the library. No, not the library, in the Year 10 room.
Boy: Oh, thanks. That's great. See you later.

2 Mum: Look, there's your geography teacher.
Girl: Mr Jones? Oh, no, where?
Mum: By the music shop. Oh, he just went in. He had a black jacket and black jeans on. He looked very nice!
Girl: Mum!
Mum: He has lovely hair.

3 Teacher: So I hope you're all ready for your history exam on Friday.
Girl: What time does it start, Mr Young?
Teacher: 9 o'clock. So please make sure you're in good time.
Boy: Er – what does 'in good time' mean? When do we need to be here?
Teacher: About fifteen minutes before. So let's say 8:45 in the main hall.

4 Boy: Are you OK?
Friend: Yeah ... well, just tired, a bit stressed ... you know all this work for the exams.
Boy: Come over later and we'll play Kung Fu Fighters.
Friend: Er ... I don't think I have the time.
Boy: Come on, it's great for stress. I play it every day. You feel much better after a game.

5 Girl: Hi Dad. Guess what? I got 81% in my science test.
Dad: That's fantastic. ... What about English?
Girl: Erm ... well, I only got 63% in English. ... But I got 75% in maths.
Dad: So, 81, 75 and 63 – that's really good. Well done!